wire jewellery

crocheted, knitted, twisted & beaded

wire jewellery
crocheted, knitted, twisted & beaded

35 stunning step-by-step projects

CHRISSIE DAY

CICO BOOKS
LONDON NEW YORK

Published by Cico Books, an imprint of
Ryland, Peters and Small
20-21 Jockey's Fields
London WC1R 4BW

ISBN-10 1-904991-46-7
ISBN-13 9-781904-991465

10 9 8 7 6 5 4 3 2 1

Designed by Janet James
Edited by Sarah Hoggett
Styled photography by Gloria Nicol
Step-by-step photography by Geoff Dann

Printed in China

CONTENTS

INTRODUCTION

Although I've always been interested in crafting, and have been knitting and working in textiles for many years, I started making wire jewelry by accident. An electrician was doing some work in my house and, while I was talking to my daughter on the phone, I picked up some scrap pieces of electrical wire and absent-mindedly began playing with them. I found I could twist and bend them into all kinds of shapes. My daughter was bemoaning the fact that she had no decent jewelry to wear for a college ball and so, purely as a joke, I made some rings and bracelets from electrical wire and sent them to her! Her friends asked her where she'd got them from—and soon I was being asked to make wire jewelry for other people, too.

From these humble, makeshift beginnings I soon realized that electrical wire was never going to give me the creative scope and potential that I was looking for. That's when I discovered how many wonderful colors of craft wire there are for jewelry making, and the fantastic ranges of beads, in all shapes and sizes—any bead worker or jewelry maker will know just how addictive they can be! Now, making wire jewelry has become a passion for me. I'm continually on the lookout for interesting beads, and am forever making sketches of colors and shapes that appeal to me, with a view to making them into pieces of jewelry. And I love experimenting, to see how far I can push the medium, and how I can combine materials and techniques in unusual ways.

Jewelry making is a very personal thing. Although I've given the type and numbers of beads that I used to make each of the pieces in this book, you may well want to adapt them to suit your own style or outfit. I've tried to include a range of projects to suit all ages and tastes—from chunky, crocheted pieces such as the Storm Bracelet on page 28 to more delicate, twisted-wire designs such as the Crystal Chandelier Earrings on page 88. I hope that you'll get as much pleasure from making—and, above all, wearing them—as I have.

Chrissie Day

Chrissie Day

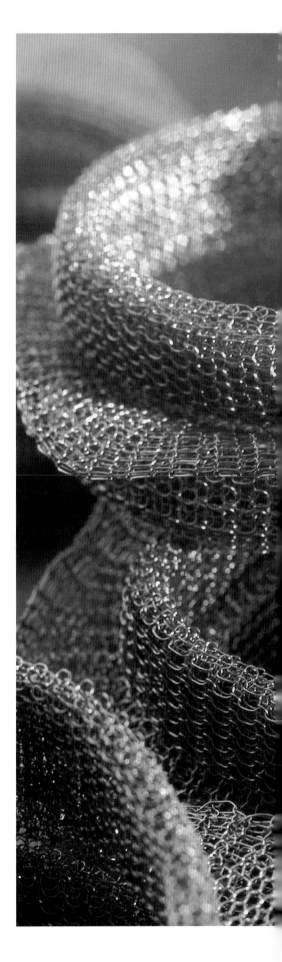

TOOLS *and* TECHNIQUES

WIRE IS AN INCREDIBLY versatile material: it comes in a wonderful array of colors and can be twisted, coiled, and shaped into so many different forms—yet it is so easy to work with. The following pages set out all the techniques and equipment you need to create such stunningly beautiful pieces of jewelry that are sure to be the envy of all your friends.

TOOLS

You actually need very few tools to make even the most complex piece. There is never any benefit not getting the correct and best tools for the job you are doing, and jewelry making is no exception to this. Learning about suppliers from fellow crafters and reading will enable you to make a good, clear choice.

However, there are a few things you should think about. Make sure that your tools sit well in your hand; comfort is paramount, and buying cheap tools is a false economy. Look for spring handles when buying tools, as they really do save on hand fatigue.

Look after your tools. When you transport them (if you're attending a class, for example), make sure they are safe and not getting damaged or doing damage. If they do not have their own storage case, a very simple one will suffice.

It is worth investing in a good set of pliers. In the suppliers list on page 124, you will find the address for a company that makes a set similar to the one I use. Funky cases are optional—but lots of fun, I think!

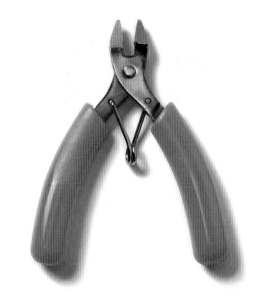

Wire cutters
There are two kinds of wire cutter—side cutters and flush cutters. Flush cutters (shown above) are better, as they cut the wire really flat, without leaving any sharp ends protruding.

Pliers
Round-nose pliers (below left) have a thin, cone-shaped body that tapers toward the end, allowing you to reach into small areas. They also allow you to make wire loops and to curl up ends of fine wire you use the tip to shape ends of wire. Flat-nose pliers (below center) are flat on the inside and allow you to grip the wire better. They are good for opening and closing loops, and for holding wire in place. You can also buy flat-nose pliers with a protective plastic cover over the jaws (below right), which are useful for straightening out wire without damaging it.

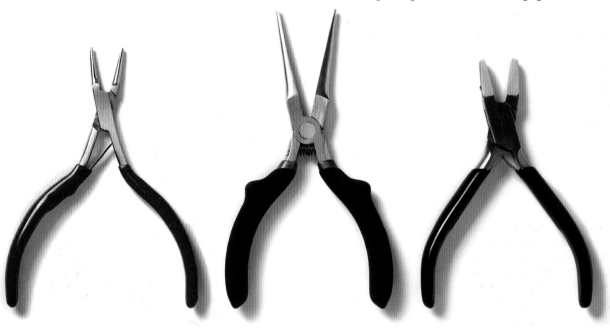

Mandrel

A mandrel (below) is a tapered metal cone, with marked gradations, that is used to shape wire to specific sizes. It is normally used for making rings and can be bought from a specialist jewelry supplier.

OTHER USEFUL TOOLS

Scissors General-purpose scissors are good for cutting pre-knit wire and cord or beading twine. Do not use them for cutting wires as this will blunt the blades.

Fine tweezers You may find it useful to buy a pair of fine tweezers for picking up small beads, but they are not essential.

Epoxy glue To seal a knot or prevent certain kinds of material from fraying, a bottle of epoxy glue is useful.

Beading needle A beading needle is like an ordinary sewing needle, but it does not taper at the end. It also has a smaller eye and is thinner, making it easier to pass through very small beads. Beading needles come in different sizes. The most popular range from size 10 (very thick) to size 15 (very fine).

Twisted-wire beading needle This is a useful tool for thread or cord that will not fit in a beading needle. It is made from twisting a length of wire back on itself, so it has no sharp point. The eye is a large, collapsible loop that allows you to thread a bead onto chunky yarn and make it small enough to fit through the bead holes.

Wire crimpers

Crimp beads are metal beads that are crushed to hold beading wire or twine. To crush them, you need a pair of wire crimpers—a special kind of plier that squeezes the bead tightly around the cord or twine. You can use flat-nose pliers, but wire crimpers have smaller jaws, making it easier to fit them into tight spaces. Above are ordinary wire crimpers (right) and micro wire crimpers (left), which is what I recommend that you use.

Bead board and bead mat

A bead board (above) or bead mat (right) is invaluable and essential for your sanity! A bead board is lined with a fabric that holds your beads in place. There is also a lip on the edge of the tray, which helps to prevent beads from rolling away. A bead mat is simply a small piece of blanketlike fabric; it, too, prevents beads from rolling around.

WIRE

Wire is available in different metals and coatings. In the projects in this book, I use both copper wire coated with enamel, and enamel wire coated with silver plate. Enamelled copper wire is less expensive than silver-plated wire. The color of the base wire affects the finished color: pink enamel applied to silver wire looks brighter than the same pink enamel applied to copper, for example.

Wire is available in many different thicknesses, or gauges, ranging from gauge 8 (the thickest) to gauge 34 (the thinnest). The lower the gauge number, the thicker the wire. Depending on the country from which you purchase it, the thickness of the wire may also be described in millimetres or in fractions on an inch. The chart on page 122 will help you convert from one system to another.

When you're choosing a wire, think about the weight of the beads or other components that you'll be using with it, as a fine wire will not be able to support a heavy component. However, you can twist two or more fine-gauge wires together to get a heavier gauge.

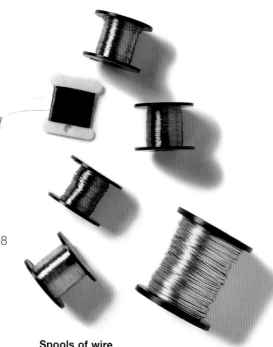

Spools of wire
Wire is sold on spools. It is worth buying large spools of the colors and gauges that you use a lot.

PRE-KNIT WIRE

Wire is also available as pre-knit tubes, sold by the yard (metre). Both fine- and coarse-knitted versions are available in two sizes—0.1mm and 0.2mm. The choice of colors is increasing all the time: you can buy pre-knit wire in all kinds of colors, from black enamelled copper to pink, gold, red, gunmetal, and silver.

Pre-knit wire is very exciting to use. It has endless possibilities: you can stretch it to widen it and make bangles or pull it in the opposite direction to create a narrower tube which, in itself, opens up even more avenues of creativity.

Coarse-knit wire
The wires shown here are coarse-knit 0.2mm. Heavier gauges retain their shape better.

Fine-knit wire
Pre-knit 0.1mm wire, shown at left, has the finest mesh. You can create lovely effects when you lay one color over another, as they modify each other and create a shimmering, two-tone appearance.

FINDINGS

Findings is a general term used to describe ready-made components such as chains, clasps, brooch bars, and earwires. They are readily available from jewelry suppliers, and craft and hobby stores.

Findings come in many different finishs—shiny and matte, antique-effect metallic, and so on. Always choose one that both complements the color of the wire and beads that you are using and the style of the piece. Magnetic clasps make a quick-and-easy fastening for a bracelet—but I never use them on necklaces for safety reasons, as other metallic objects can sometimes be attracted to the magnet.

Clasps are available in many different designs and finishes. Choose one that complements the style and color of the piece that you are making.

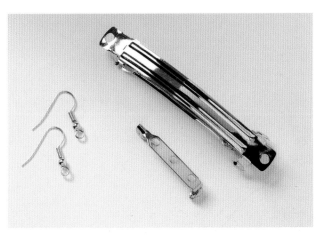

Ready-made earwires, brooch bars, and barrettes can easily be decorated with beaded wires in the colors of your choice.

You can attach beaded wires, or pre-knit wire, to silver (or silver-plated) choker rings for a simple but stylish piece of jewelry.

BEADS

Beads are seductive! Walking into any bead supply store is like entering another world. Your brain will reel from trying to take it all in—so just stand back and enjoy it!

Sometimes the sight of a new range of beads is enough to fire my mind and a design springs from a particular bead. At other times, sketches that I have made previously will suddenly match up with a new-found treasure. Color is where everything starts. You will find yourself drawn to your own favorite color range but as an artist you should try every so often to select colors that you have not tried before—you may surprise yourself.

On page 124, you will find a list of the bead suppliers that I have chosen to use. I also commission specialist bead makers to make beads for me; their websites, too, are listed on page 124. But there are many more suppliers for you to discover for yourself. One visit to an internet search engine will reveal many sources. Do not forget, however, that if you purchase beads from overseas, you may be charged import duty and tax. It is always good to contact these firms before you buy and ask if they already have a supplier in your own country.

Pearl beads
Pearl beads come in a variety of shapes, sizes, and finishes, from "rice" pearls (which look like grains of rice) and "potatoes" (which are irregularly shaped) to rounds. They may be freshwater or cultured, and will be priced accordingly.

Oriental crystal beads
Crystal beads produced in the Far East tend to be less expensive than those from the Czech Republic and Austria. They may not have the same clarity and sparkle, but they are are useful additions to your bead stash.

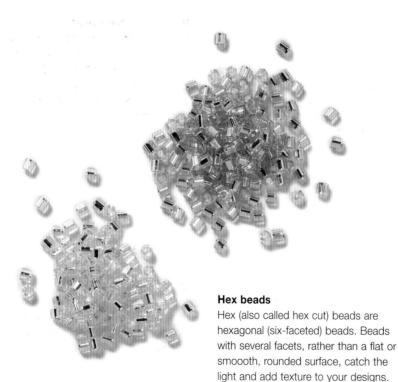

Hex beads
Hex (also called hex cut) beads are hexagonal (six-faceted) beads. Beads with several facets, rather than a flat or smoooth, rounded surface, catch the light and add texture to your designs.

Glass cube beads

Glass cube beads are made by feeding a rod of glass into a machine, which inserts a needle through the center to form a hole and then cuts the rod to size.

Glass cane beads

A "cane" is a rod of glass. Sometimes, as here, several canes of different colors may be built up to make a larger cane, which is then extruded to form beads.

Czech two-tone crystal beads

The Czech Republic has a long history of producing high-quality crystal. Crystal beads such as these add an incomparable sparkle to your jewelry making.

Hand-made glass beads

The island of Murano, near Venice, has been a glass-making center for centuries and still produces high-quality glass beads. They can be expensive—but I think they're worth it for a really special piece of jewelry!

Seed beads

"Seed bead" is a generic term for any small bead. They are usually round in shape and range in size from under a millimetre to several millimetres.

Hand-made polymer clay beads

Beads can be made from all kinds of materials, including polymer clay. The beads shown here are hand painted and would make a lovely focal point for a chunky necklace or bracelet.

Crimp beads

Crimp beads are tiny metal beads that are crushed to hold beading wire or twine. They are normally applied next to clasps.

BEAD CHARTS

The charts here enable you to work out how many beads of different sizes you will need to complete your designs.

SEED BEADS

Seed beads, particularly from the Czech Republic, are often sold from the factories by the hank (a hank being twelve 20-in./50-cm strands, or strings). One advantage of this is that if the beads are on a strand you know each one definitely has a hole in the middle. When the beads are sold by retailers, the hanks are often broken down into bags of a particular weight —and the retailer should be able to tell you roughly how many beads are in the packet.

If you are buying strands, or hanks, of beads the chart below will enable you to calculate how many seed beads you need for your chosen design.

Note that, with seed beads, the size refers not to the length of the bead but to the size of the hole. (In addition, the smaller the number, the bigger the seed bead—so a size 6 seed bead is bigger than a size 16 seed bead.)

Size	Approx. no. of beads on one 20-in. (50-cm) strand	Approx. no. of beads per inch/2.5cm	Approx. diameter of one bead in mm
6	175	9	4.0
8	240	12	3.1
9	263	13	2.7
10	295	15	2.5
11	340	17	2.1
12	370	20	1.9
13	415	21	1.7
14	465	24	1.6
16	560	28	1.3

APPROXIMATE NUMBER OF BEADS IN STANDARD BAG SIZES

Beads retailers often sell bags of beads by weight. The chart (above right) shows roughly how many beads of a particular type you can expect to find in a standard bag.

Typical bead type	Approximate bag size	Number of beads
11–seed	20 g	2,000
11–delica	5 g	1,000
3.3 mm delica	5 g	150
13–seed	20 g	3,000
14–seed	20 g	5,150
15–hex-cut	20 g	5,880
20–seed	3 g	2,800
25–hex-cut	20 g	960
11–pony bead	10 g	150
11–triangle	20 g	2,000
4 mm cube	20 g	215
3 mm bugle	20 g	1,770
5 mm bugle	20 g	770
9 mm bugle	20 g	500
12 mm bugle	20 g	250

CALCULATE THE BEADS YOU NEED

There's nothing more infuriating than finding you don't have enough beads to finish a project. Here's how to work out how many beads you need before you start.

Work out the length of your wire or cord. (If working in inches, multiply the number of inches by 25.4 to find the length in millimetres.) Then divide the length of the wire or cord in mm by the length of one bead (in mm) to find out how many beads you need.

For example, to work out how many beads you need for a 16-inch (406-mm) strand of 4mm beads:

- 16 x 25.4 = 406.4
- 406.4 ÷ 4mm (the length of one bead) = 101.6
- Rounding up the fraction of a bead, you will need 102 4mm beads to fill a 16-inch strand.

The first column in the table on the right shows the number of beads of different sizes in 1 in. (2.5 cm). The next two columns show the approximate number of beads in two standard sizes of strands (16 in./40 cm and 24 in./60 cm), rounded up to the nearest whole number.

Bead length mm	Number of beads per inch (2.5 cm)	Number of beads in 16 inches (40 cm)	Number of beads in 24 inches (60 cm)
3	8.50	135	203
4	6.25	102	153
5	5.00	82	122
6	4.25	68	102
7	3.50	58	87
8	3.25	51	76
9	2.75	45	68
10	2.5	41	61
11	2.25	37	56
12	2.00	34	51
14	1.75	29	44
16	1.50	26	38
18	1.50	23	34
20	1.25	21	31

COLOR AND DESIGN

As you will see from the projects in this book, I take a lot of the inspiration for my jewelry pieces from things that I see around me, whether it's summer berries, dew, or raindrops glistening on a flower, or colors reflected in the sea. Sometimes I only have time to dash the colors into my sketchbook, with a quick note about what I saw. I can remember a scene but not always the exact colors—so recording them becomes a priority.

The design for a piece of jewelry may not come until much later—but keeping a sketchbook and making a note of the colors or shapes that you like is an invaluable discipline for any designer, regardless of what medium he or she is working in.

I know, however, that color is something that many people are afraid of. Buying a good color book and learning a little about color theory will pay dividends and increase your satisfaction with the work that you produce. Your work will not always be to your liking, but do not consider the items a failure: rather, see them as experimental pieces made on a learning curve.

That is only part of the story. Buying a good color wheel is very helpful when it comes to choosing colors that will work well together—but there is really no substitute for hands-on experimentation. Even when you put together two colors of bead that should, theoretically, look fantastic, you can often find that something doesn't look quite right. It may be the finish of the bead—opaque versus translucent, matte versus shiny, for example. And for me, that hands-on experimentation is all part of the joy of making jewelry: beads are incredibly beautiful and seductive-looking things, and often, when I have got a few minutes to spare, I just take out a few handfuls and play around with them, putting one color and shape next to another to see what happens. Try it and see!

I was making a dessert using summer fruits one day and was struck by the lovely colors. They inspired me to make the Summer Berries Brooch on page 34. I started by making a rough sketch in felt-tip pen to work out the relative proportions of each color. The angular shapes of the beads helped to represent the individual seeds of the berries and also gave the design a graphic quality that reminded me of the work of Charles Rennie Mackintosh, like the cover of the notepad (above).

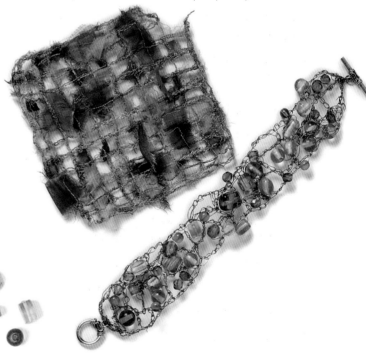

Colors in the sea inspired me to make the Sea-blue Bracelet on page 32. Initially, I was going to make a textile piece—but then it struck me that the approach would work equally well with a crocheted mesh of wire as the base.

COLOR TERMINOLOGY

Although there isn't space here to go into detail about color theory, the following definitions may help you to make sense of a number of the terms that you may come across.

Achromatic colors: whites, blacks, and grays.

Adjacent colors: colors that are next to one another on the color wheel.

Analogous color scheme: a color scheme that uses adjacent colors.

Brightness: this tells us how strong a color is. For example, colors such as white and yellow have a high brightness; browns and grays have a medium brightness; and black has a low brightness.

Cold colors: blues, greens, and violets.

Complementary colors: colors that are opposite one another on the color wheel, such as red and green. Complementary colors generally work well together.

Hue: another word for a color.

Monochromatic color scheme: a color scheme that uses only one color (or tints, tones, and shades of one color).

Primary colors: the three colors from which all others arise (red, yellow, and blue).

Saturation: a term used to describe the purity or intensity of a color. A highly saturated color is vivid and intense, while a less saturated color appears more muted and gray.

Secondary colors: colors created by mixing two primary colors together (for example, mixing blue and yellow together gives the secondary color of green).

Shade: a color to which black has been added.

Tertiary color: a color created by mixing two secondary colors, or one secondary and one primary color, together.

Tint: a color to which white has been added.

Tone: the relative lightness or darkness of a color.

Value: another word for tone.

Warm color: reds, oranges, and yellows.

SOME TIPS ON USING COLOR

Color is very subjective: we all have our favorite color combinations—and ultimately, if you like what you've done, that's all that matters. However, there are a few things that you should think about when selecting wire and beads.

- Choose beads in a color that complements your wire rather than competes with it.

- Think of the look you are trying to create—contemporary or period—and choose your color combinations accordingly.

- Consider the finish of a bead. Is it matte or shiny, for example? What about its luminosity—does it radiate light?

- White can have a magical effect; it is an indispensable color and adjoining colors are transformed when you add white to a piece.

- Analogous colors give a subtle design.

- By using contrasting (or complementary) colors, you will create a bold piece.

- We tend to be more sensitive to changes in hue than to changes in brightness—and more sensitive to changes in brightness than to changes in saturation.

BASIC TECHNIQUES

Making wire jewelry may appear complicated, but in practice it really is very easy. As you have seen, the equipment you need is minimal—and a few very basic techniques, show here, will take you a long way.

GENERAL TECHNIQUES

The following techniques are ones that you will find useful for all kinds of wire jewelry.

Picking up beads on wire

When you have a lot of small seed beads to thread onto wire, it would be virtually impossible to pick each one up and thread it on individually. Instead, try this simple scooping technique.

Lay the beads in a pile on a bead mat, so that they cannot roll away. Push the end of the wire into the pile and "scoop" the beads onto it, using your free hand to keep the remaining beads in a neat pile on the mat.

Attaching a clasp

When you've spent a lot of time making a necklace or a bracelet, the last thing you want is for the clasp to detach itself from the piece. Here's how to make sure it's firmly anchored.

1 When you've finished making your piece of jewelry, leave about 3 or 4 inches (7–10 cm) of wire uncut at the end. Thread the clasp onto this wire and push it down as far as it will go. Loop the wire over the clasp and through the end of the piece of jewelry.

2 Using the wire like a sewing thread, "stitch" the clasp into position, taking the wire over the clasp and back through the end of the piece of jewelry eight or nine times until it is firmly anchored. Snip off any excess wire with your wire cutters and, if necessary, press the end of the wire with flat-nose pliers so that no sharp ends are left sticking out.

CROCHETING WITH WIRE

Crocheting with wire is surprisingly easy to do and the techniques is exactly the same as when crocheting with yarn. Keep your stitches fairly loose, so that you can easily slide the hook through them. Experiment with different thicknesses of wire and sizes of hook to see what effects you can create.

Crimping beads

Crimp beads are normally used with bracelet fastenings. They provide a neater finish than simply twisting any protruding wires around each other.

Making a foundation chain

All crochet work begins with a foundation chain, into which you then work subsequent rows of stitches.

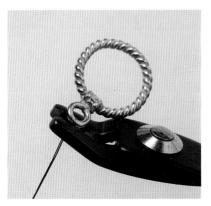

1 Feed the crimp bead onto the wire and push it as close to the clasp as possible. Feed the wire back through the crimp bead.

1 About 6 in. (15 cm) from the end of the wire, make a loop and insert your crochet hook.

2 Wrap the wire counterclockwise around the hook, forming a second loop on the hook.

2 Using micro wire crimpers, press the bead to tighten its hold on the wire. Snip off any excess wire to finish, cutting as close as possible to the bead.

3 Draw the second loop through the first one and pull taut to make the first stitch.

4 Repeat Steps 2 and 3 until the foundation chain has the required number of stitches.

Slip stitch

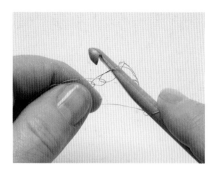

1 Make a foundation chain and insert the hook into the second chain from the hook.

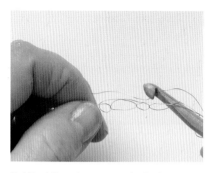

2 Wrap the wire counterclockwise around the hook.

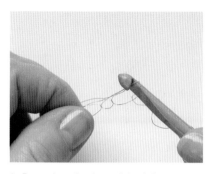

3 Draw the wire through both loops to make the stitch.

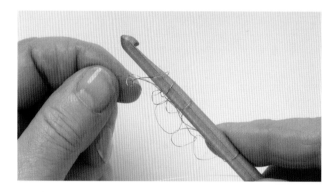

4 Repeat Steps 1 through 3, working one slip stitch into each chain on the foundation row.

Single crochet stitch

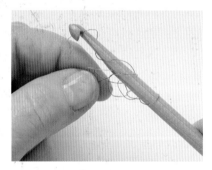

1 Make a foundation chain of the required length. Insert the hook into the second chain from the hook, and wrap the wire counterclockwise around the hook.

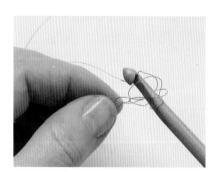

2 Draw the hook back through the work.

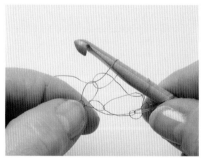

3 Wrap the wire counterclockwise around the hoop again, and draw the hook through all three loops on the hook.

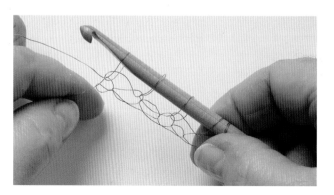

4 Repeat Steps 1 through 3 until you reach the end of the row.

Double crochet stitch

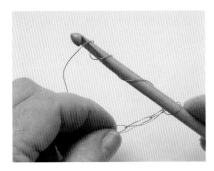

1 Make a foundation chain of the required length. Wrap the wire counterclockwise twice around the hook.

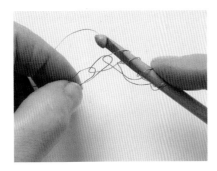

2 Insert the hook into the fifth chain from the hook.

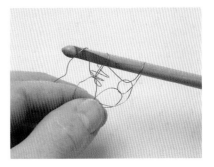

3 Wrap the wire counterclockwise around the hook again, and draw the hook through the first loop only.

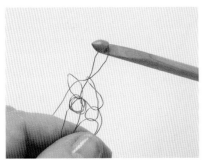

4 Wrap the wire again, and draw the hook through the next loop. Wrap the wire again, and draw the hook through the last loop on the hook.

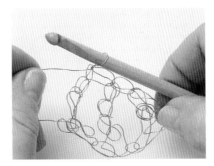

5 Repeat Step 3 in each chain until you reach the end of the row.

Binding off

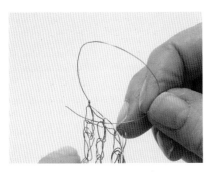

1 Cut the wire, leaving a tail about 6 in. (15 cm) long. Push the tail of wire through all the loops on the last row of stitches.

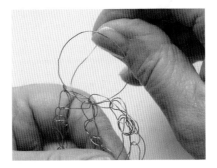

2 Pull taut. Cut off any excess wire.

KNITTING WITH WIRE

The techniques for knitting with wire are, with the exception of binding off, exactly the same as those you would use when knitting with yarn.

Casting on

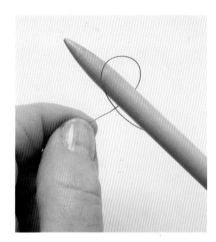

1 Make a small loop in the wire and insert the needle.

2 Wrap the wire clockwise around the top of the needle.

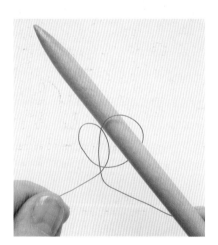

3 Using your fingers, lift the first loop over the second and let it drop off the needle as shown above.

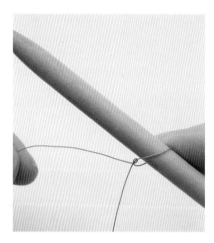

4 Pull to tighten. Repeat until you have cast on the required number of stitches.

Knit stitch

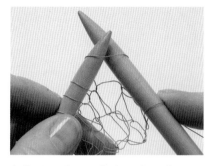

1 Cast on the required number of stitches. Hold the needle with the cast-on stitches in your left hand. Insert the right needle into the front of the first cast-on stitch from left to right.

2 Wrap the wire around the tip of the right-hand needle, so that it rests between the two needles.

3 Bring the right needle under the wrapped-around wire and gently slide it toward the right.

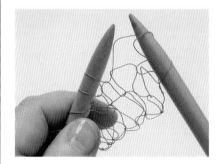

4 Gently slip the stitch off the left needle and onto the right needle.

Decreasing stitches

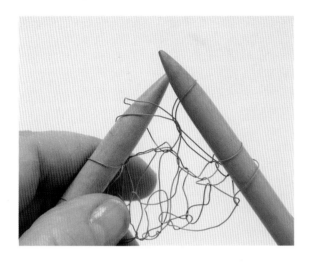

1 Insert the needle through the first two stitches on the left needle. Work a knit stitch, slipping both stitches off the left needle at the same time.

Increasing stitches

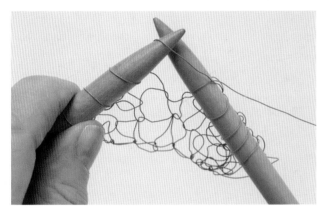

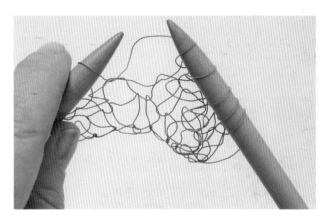

1 Knit into the front of the stitch and wrap the wire around the tip of the needle, as usual, but do not slip the stitch off the needle. Knit into the back of the same stitch.

2 Complete the stitch and slip both stitches off the needle at the same time.

Binding off

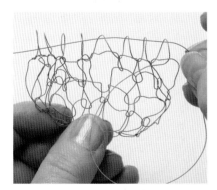

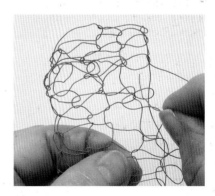

1 Cut the wire off the spool, leaving enough to go through all the knitting. Gently slide your knitting off the needle.

2 Pull the wire through all the stitches, and press down to flatten.

3 Using your fingers, "overstitch" the excess wire through the stitches and pull it taut.

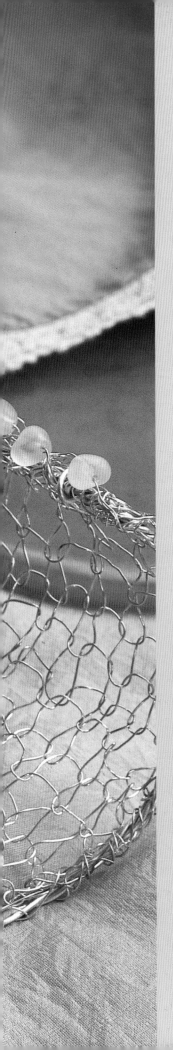

CHAPTER 1

CROCHETED
and KNITTED
WIRE JEWELRY

IT MAY COME as a surprise to learn that you can crochet and knit with wire, just as you can with yarn, but the effects are stunning. Depending on the stitch and size of needle or hook you choose, you can create a tightly woven fabric or an open mesh, into which you can incorporate as many or as few beads as you wish for extra sparkle.

The colors in this bracelet were inspired by seeing sunshine glinting on wet paving stones. To work out how long to make the bracelet, measure around your wrist and add ½ in. (1 cm). Subtract the length of the clasp from the previous total. Draw a line to this measurement on a piece of paper. As you crochet, check the length of your work against the line and stop at the appropriate point.

STORM BRACELET

MATERIALS

D-3 (3-mm) crochet hook

20–30 black-and-white and gold glass cane beads
in various sizes

1 spool of 24-gauge (0.3-mm) gunmetal bronze wire

Antique-silver T-clasp

Bead mat

Wire cutters

TECHNIQUE

Double crochet stitch (see page 22)

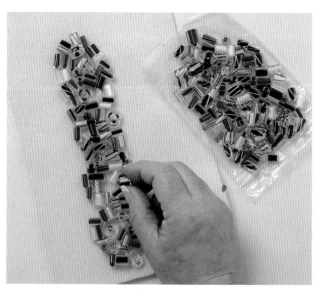

1 Lay around 20–30 beads on a bead mat and move them around until you get a design that you like. Look at the color distribution and the shapes and make sure you don't get too many of the same type of bead clustered close together. The larger beads should be nearer the center than the edge.

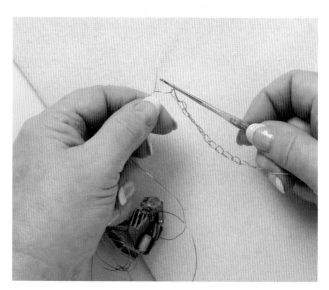

2 Working from the spool, thread the beads onto 24-gauge (0.3-mm) gunmetal bronze wire. Remember that the last beads that you thread onto the wire will be the ones that you work with first—so thread them on in reverse order, starting from the end of the bracelet.

3 Using a size D-3 (3-mm) crochet hook and starting about 6 in. (15 cm) from the end of the wire, work a foundation row of 14 chains (see page 21). This will be the width of the bracelet.

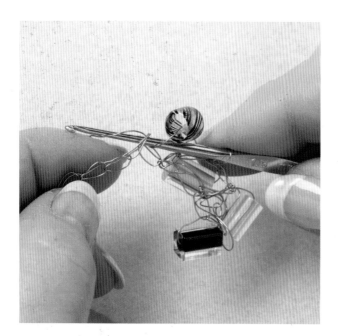

4 Take up the first bead and work 1 double crochet stitch (see page 23) into the third chain of the foundation row. Continue working 1 double crochet stitch into each chain, working in one bead every second or third stitch, until the first row is complete.

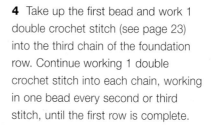

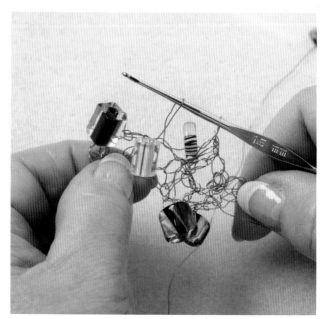

5 Turn the work. Continue working rows of double crochet stitch, interspersing one bead every second or third stitch, until the bracelet is long enough to fit around your wrist.

6 When the bracelet is the required length, cut the wire off the spool leaving about 6 in. (15 cm) at the end. Take the loose end of wire to the center of one end of the bracelet and, using your fingers, weave it in and out of the crochet stitches to secure it, ready to attach the clasp.

7 Thread one section of the T-clasp onto the protruding wire and weave it in and out of the bracelet three or four times to secure it. Snip off any excess wire, making sure that there is no sharp end protruding. Repeat at the other end of the bracelet with the other section of the T-clasp.

BEDAZZLING BRACELETS
Brightly colored beads make striking bracelets that are equally suitable for day and evening wear.

On vacation in Corfu, I looked down into the ocean from a mountainside road and saw the most spectacular mixture of greens and turquoises. The image stayed in my mind and I used it to create the color scheme for this bracelet.

SEA-BLUE BRACELET

MATERIALS

24-gauge (0.5-mm) green wire

Approx. 30 green and blue-green glass beads,
3–5-mm in diameter

B-1 (2-mm) crochet hook

T-clasp

Bead mat

TECHNIQUE

Double crochet stitch (see page 23)

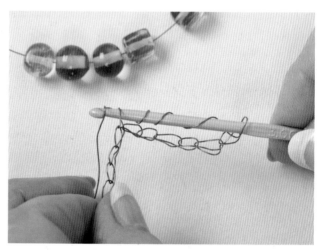

1 Lay out about 30 beads on a bead mat and move them around until you get a design that you like. Working from the spool, thread the beads onto 24-gauge (0.5-mm) green wire. Using a size B-1 (2-mm) crochet hook and starting about 6 in. (15 cm) from the end of the wire, work a foundation row the length that you want the width of the bracelet to be to the nearest multiple of 3, plus 6 chains. Work 1 double crochet stitch (see page 23) into the 6th chain.

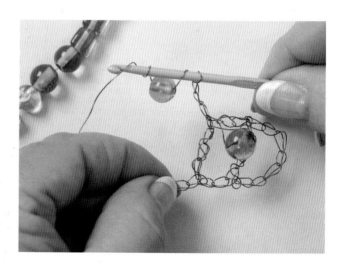

2 Work 3 chains, miss 3 chains, take up one bead, and work 1 double stitch (see right). Repeat until you reach the end of the foundation chain.

3 Turn the work. Work 6 chains. Pull up one bead, and work 1 double stitch into the first stitch of the first row. * Work 3 chains, take up one bead, and work 1 double stitch into the next stitch of the first row. Repeat from * until you reach the end of the row, adding beads only on alternate rows.

4 Continue until the bracelet is the desired length. (Depending on the size of your wrist, this is normally about 14 rows.) Cut the wire off the spool, leaving about 6 in. (15 cm). Take the loose end of wire to the center of one end of the bracelet and, using your fingers, weave it in and out of the crochet stitches several times to secure it, just as you would when securing sewing stitches. Thread one section of the T-clasp onto the protruding wire and weave it in and out of the bracelet three or four time to secure it. Snip off any excess wire, making sure no sharp end protrudes. Repeat at the other end of the bracelet with the other section of the T-clasp.

Mixing summer fruits to make a dessert one summer's day inspired me to make my color selection for this piece. The crocheted mesh is made using three strands of wire simultaneously, which gives a tighter mesh than using only one wire. It is then rolled into a flower-bud shape with a beaded stamen. The cube-shaped beads echo the shape of the mesh and create a regular shape.

SUMMER BERRIES BROOCH

MATERIALS

3 spools of 24-gauge (0.5-mm) wire in colors to match the stones

1 tube 4-mm glass cube beads in a mix of summer-berry colors

B-1 (2-mm) crochet hook

Brooch finding with 3 holes

TECHNIQUE

Double crochet stitch (see page 23)

1 Working from the spools, thread a selection of glass cube beads onto your three chosen colors of wire, covering about 18 in. (45 cm) of wire.

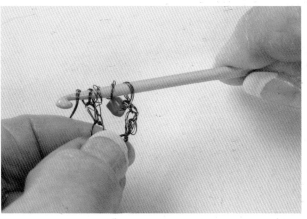

2 Starting about 6 in. (15 cm) from the ends of the wires, work a foundation chain of 9 chains, and then work 5 more chains (see page 21). * Take up 1 glass cube bead, and work 1 double stitch into the 6th chain. Work 1 chain, then repeat from * until you reach the end of the foundation row.

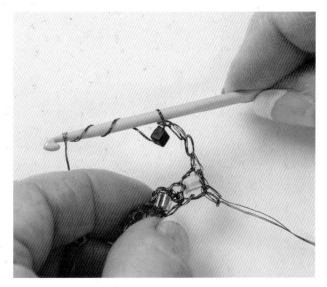 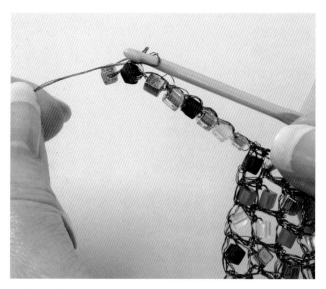

3 Turn the work, work 4 chains, take up 1 glass cube bead, and work 1 double stitch into the first stitch of the first row. Continue working double stitches, working 1 chain between each stitch, until you have completed 9 rows.

4 Work 13 slip stitches (see page 22), taking up 1 bead with each stitch. (This forms the stamen of the flower.) Bind off (see page 23).

5 Fold the stamen diagonally over the center of the square mesh, then roll the mesh across it to form a tapered cone.

6 Feed the loose end of wire left at the start of Step 2 through to the back of the flower. Weave it in and out of the holes in the brooch finding to secure the flower.

The flower "stamen" is made by working a chain of 13 beads at one corner of the crocheted and beaded square.

BLUEBELL BROOCH
My color choice for this brooch was inspired by bluebell flowers—a herald of spring and warmer days to come.

This design was inspired by looking at sand and stones all mingled together on a Scottish beach after a winter storm. The colors reminded me of a passage in a book that I'd read, which described the depth of colors in a witch's brew.

MAGIC PEBBLE EARRINGS

MATERIALS

24-gauge (0.5-mm) black and gunmetal bronze wires

20–24 green, gray, black, and clear glass beads

B-1 (2-mm) crochet hook

Bead mat

Ready-made earwires

Wire cutters

TECHNIQUE

Slip stitch (see page 22)

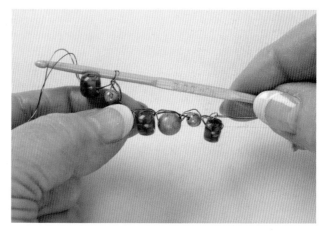

1 To make the earrings, lay out two identical rows of 10–12 beads on your bead mat. Holding both spools of wire together in your hand and using a size B-1 (2mm) crochet hook, work 11 chains for the foundation row (see page 21). * Take up 1 bead, then work 1 slip stitch into the first chain, adding one bead into every stitch. Repeat from * until you reach the end of the row.

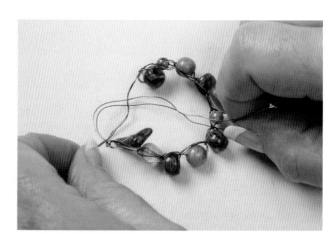

2 Cut the wires off the spool, leaving about 2 in. (5 cm) at each end. Join the two ends in a knot to form a circle.

MAGIC PEBBLE BRACELET

To make a matching bracelet, use a thicker wire (21-gauge/0.7-mm wire) and a size D-3 (3-mm) crochet hook. Place the beads on the wire as described in the instructions for the earrings, and take one bead into every single slip stitch until the bracelet is the length you require, remembering to take into account the length of the clasp.

3 Twist the protruding wires together.

4 Feed the twisted wires through the earwire until they are about ¼ in. (0.5 cm) above the bead circle.

5 Wrap the wire around itself to secure, finishing by wrapping it tightly around the first bead in the circle. Repeat Steps 1 through 5 to make the second earring.

I always like to experiment with new knitting yarns when they are released and this ribbon yarn combines really well with wire. I am interested in the Edwardian period and the designs of that time, so it seemed natural to design a choker—a typically Edwardian piece of jewelry.

EDWARDIAN CHOKER

MATERIALS

24-gauge (0.5-mm) brown wire

Ribbon yarn

Size 19 (16-mm) knitting needles

Size 4 (3.5-mm) knitting needles

Polymer clay feature bead, 1½ in. (4 cm) long

3-mm double delica beads in shiny bronze, old gold and shiny petrel

5–7mm round gold or bronze bead

TECHNIQUE

Knit stitch (see page 24)

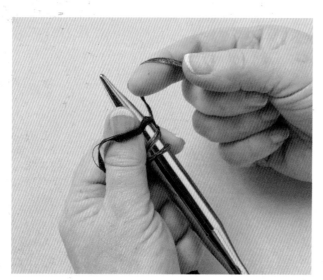

1 Tie the ends of the brown wire and ribbon yarn together. Using size 19 (16-mm) knitting needles, cast on 5 stitches (see page 24).

2 Knit the number of rows required to fit your neck, minus the measurement of the polymer clay bead. Fasten off, leaving about 4 in. (10 cm) at the end. This forms the basic choker.

3 Now make the circular disks that decorate the choker. Tie the ends of the brown wire and ribbon yarn together again, as in Step 1. Using size 4 (3.5-mm) knitting needles, cast on 5 stitches (see page 24). Knit 6 rows, increasing 1 stitch at the beginning of each row (see page 25). Knit 6 rows. Knit 6 rows, decreasing 1 stitch at the beginning of each row (see page 25) until you are left with 5 stitches. Bind off (see page 25). Make three disks in this way.

4 Space the disks evenly along the choker, making sure that the cast-on edge lies at the bottom of the choker. When you are happy with the position, anchor the disks in place by weaving the loose ends of wire and yarn at the top and bottom of each disk in and out of the choker several times. Snip off any excess wire and yarn, and press the ends firmly into the choker with your pliers to make sure that no sharp ends protrude.

5 At the cast-on end of the choker, twist the wire and yarn together and thread through to the center of the end of the choker to form a loop.

6 Wrap the end of the wire-and-yarn twist around the loop and weave it in and out of the choker several times to secure. Snip off any excess, and press the end firmly into the choker with your pliers to make sure that no sharp ends protrude.

7 At the fastened-off end of the choker, twist the wire and yarn together, as in Step 5, and thread through to the center of the end of the choker. Thread on the polymer clay feature bead, then weave the wire-and-yarn twist in and out of the choker several times to secure it. Snip off any excess, and press the end firmly into the choker with your pliers to make sure that no sharp ends protrude.

8 Cut about 18 in. (45 cm) of 24-gauge (0.5-mm) brown wire and anchor it along the bottom of the choker. Pick up 2 or 3 double delica beads on the wire, and push them along to the end of the wire so that they sit on the front of the choker, along the bottom edge.

9 Take the wire through to the back of the choker to anchor the beads. Bring it back through to the front, pick up another small group of beads, and attach them in the same way. Continue until you have beaded the whole of the bottom of the choker, attaching groups of 2 or 3 beads randomly wherever you want a bit of extra sparkle.

10 Knot a 5–7-mm round gold or bronze bead onto the cast-on length of yarn and wire, then knot the yarn and wire immediately below the bead to hold it in place.

RASPBERRY-LIME CHOKER

For a summery alternative, combine two strands of 24-gauge (0.5-mm) wire (raspberry pink and lime green) with two strands of fine pink and lime-green mohair yarn.

The stripes can be any depth you choose. Using a very fine black wire in the center creates the illusion that the beads are simply suspended in thin air.

STRIPED CUFF

MATERIALS

19-gauge (0.9-mm) champagne-colored wire

28-gauge (0.3-mm) champagne-colored wire

32-gauge (0.2-mm) black wire

Size 9 and 11 seed beads

Size I (5.5-mm) knitting needles

Wire cutters

Flat-nose pliers

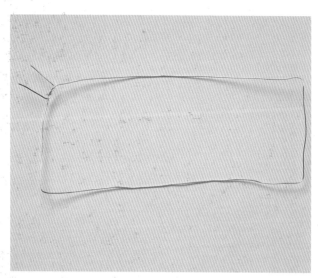

1 Measure around your wrist, add the depth of the bracelet, and multiply by two. Cut a length of 19-gauge (0.9-mm) champagne-colored wire to this measurement and shape it into a rectangle. Twist the loose ends of wire together.

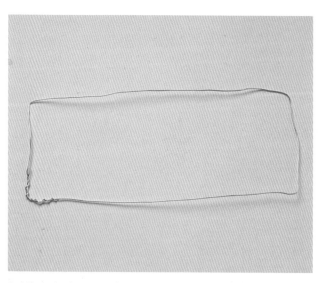

2 Wrap the loose ends around the rectangular frame several times and squeeze them with your flat-nose pliers so that no sharp ends stick out.

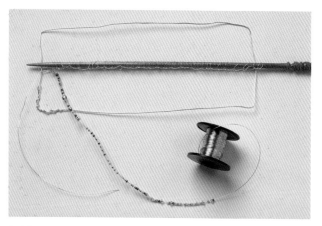

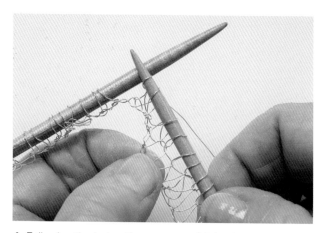

3 Thread about 90 seed beads onto the end of a spool of 28-gauge (0.3-mm) champagne-colored wire. Using size I (5.5-mm) knitting needles and the same spool of wire, cast on enough stitches to fill the length of the bracelet (see page 24).

4 Following the instructions on page 24, begin knitting. It will look strange and misshapen to begin with, but just keep tweaking it into shape with your fingers.

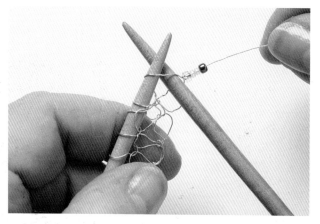

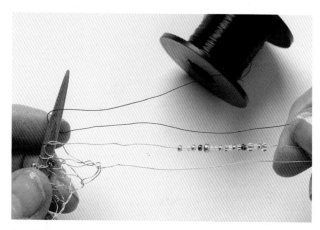

5 Every four or five stitches, draw 2–4 beads up to the work and work a knit stitch around them as normal.

6 When you have completed about an inch (2.5 cm) of knitting, change to 32-gauge (0.2-mm) black wire. Hold the two colors of wire together at the top of the work, leaving a long tail. Twist the wires together, and recommence knitting, using the black wire as your "yarn."

7 Continue knitting with the black wire, again adding in beads wherever you wish, until the black stripe is the depth that you want.

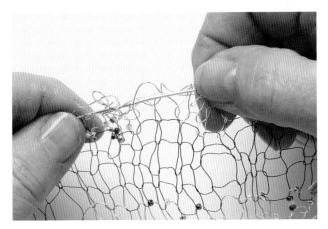

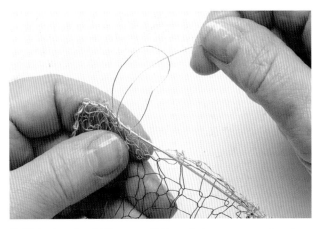

8 If you wish, add in another stripe of champagne-colored wire, changing the colors as described in Step 5. When the knitting is the depth required to fill the bracelet, bind off (see page 25). Stretch the knitted wire over the rectangular frame that you made in Step 1, and bend the edges over the edge of the frame.

9 Cut a length of 28-gauge (0.3-mm) champagne-colored wire, and "overstitch" the knitting in place, looping the wire over the frame and through the knitting. Bend the frame to fit the bracelet around your wrist.

CRYSTAL-EDGED CUFF
Attaching crystal beads around the frame provides an eye-catching finishing touch.

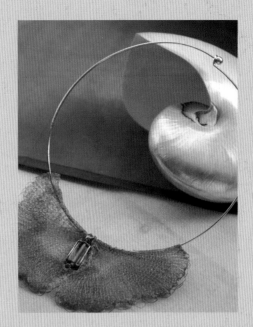

CHAPTER 2

PRE-KNIT WIRE JEWELRY

PRE-KNIT WIRE is a relatively recent innovation, but it's incredibly easy to work with. You can roll or fold it in your fingers to create a dense, tight mesh; stretch and pull it to form interesting shapes; and work one color over another to create a lovely, shimmering effect. If you're looking for really quick-and-easy jewelry projects that you can make in a matter of minutes, then the pieces in this chapter are a good place to start.

This piece was inspired by my reading about Egyptian history and jewelry traditions. The shape of the choker is straight out of Ancient Egypt, while the geometric pattern of the decoration is pure Art Deco.

EGYPTIAN CHOKER

MATERIALS

0.2-mm coarse black pre-knit wire

32-gauge (0.2-mm) black wire

Needle

3 8–10-mm long hematite beads

35 3-mm oblong black beads

1 Cut a 40-in. (1-m) length of 0.2-mm coarse black pre-knit wire and fold it in half lengthwise, making sure the edges align exactly. Press hard with your fingers. Fold under the raw short ends. Thread a needle with 32-gauge (0.2-mm) black wire and slipstitch the ends to close them. Measure the width of the pre-knit wire plus 1 in. (2.5 cm) from one end, and make a sharp crease with your fingers. This will become the loop through which you feed the rest of the choker.

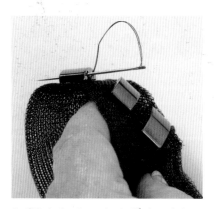

2 Stitch the three hematite beads in place, making sure they fit within the crease marks.

3 Stitch the black oblong beads along the lower edge of the choker (the unfolded long edge), spacing them evenly and making sure that your stitches go through both layers of the pre-knit wire.

4 Fold the wire along the crease mark for the loop that you made in Step 1, and slipstitch along the edge, stitching through both layers on the folded-over section but only through the back layer of the choker, so that the stitches do not show on the front.

DECORATED LOOP CHOKERS

Decorate the loops any way you choose, usiing either a single large bead or several smaller ones arranged in a geometric pattern—but use beads that are similar to the wire in color and tone, to maintain the subtlety of the design.

In the Art Deco period that followed the First World War, there was a reaction against unnecessary decoration. Jewelry assumed simple lines, accentuated by dazzling bursts of vivid, contrasting primary colors—hence the bold contrasts of this matching necklace and bracelet.

ART DECO JEWELRY SET

MATERIALS

0.2-mm coarse pre-knit silver wire

0.2-mm coarse pre-knit red wire

Approx. 10 3-mm Czech crystals

Approx. 20 3-mm glass cube beads

Cotton thread and needle

Scissors

NECKLACE

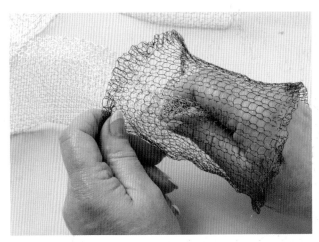

1 Cut a piece of 0.2-mm coarse pre-knit silver wire to the length you require plus about 1 in. (2.5 cm) and a 5-in. (12.5-cm) length of 0.2-mm coarse pre-knit red wire. Open out the tube of red pre-knit wire and slip it over the silver, centering it on the length.

2 Roll the pre-knit wires in your hands to mesh them together.

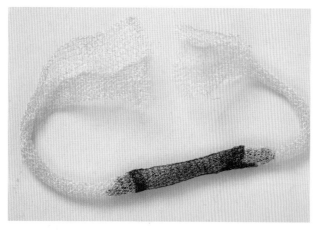

3 Leaving about 2 in. (5 cm) unrolled at each end, continue rolling the wire until the necklace is an even thickness all the way along.

4 Tie a knot in the red section.

5 Place one open end of the silver wire inside the other.

6 Roll the ends, as in Step 2, to mesh the wires together.

7 Thread a needle with cotton thread and stitch glass beads and crystals onto the central red portion, taking the thread all the way through to the back of the knot and back up to the front again to secure the beads in place.

BRACELET

Here, I reversed the colors, using silver as the contrast color. The bracelet is rolled in exactly the same way as the necklace, but you need to add the clasp before you add the contrast color.

1 Cut about 10 or 11 in. (25–28 cm) of red pre-knit wire and roll it, as for the necklace. Roll each end to a fine point. Insert each end into one half of a magnetic clasp.

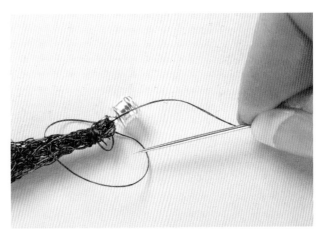

2 Bend the protruding wire over the top of the clasp and stitch it firmly in place.

3 Undo the clasp. Take a 3-in. (7-cm) length of silver pre-knit wire and slip it over the bracelet, centering it on the length (as shown above).

4 Roll as before, in order to mesh the wires together.

SILVER DREAM SET
Silver and black wires make a stunning jewelry set for extra-special occasions.

Formal balls in 19th-century Russia and the romance of dressing for the occasion inspired me to make this piece.

RUSSIAN WINTER NECKLACE

MATERIALS

0.1-mm coarse pre-knit gunmetal wire

Scissors

Magnetic clasp

Needle and thread

32-gauge (0.2-mm) wire

Seed beads—mix of bronze, bottle green, and turquoise

Stone in a mount

Wire cutters

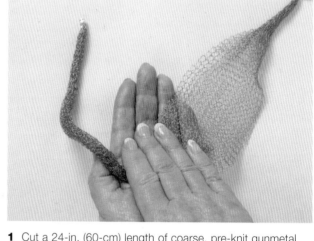

1 Cut a 24-in. (60-cm) length of coarse, pre-knit gunmetal wire. Roll each end to a fine point and insert it into one half of a magnetic clasp. Bend the protruding wire over the top of the clasp and stitch it in place. Roll the whole necklace until it forms a tight mesh and is an even thickness along its length.

2 Cut a length of 32-gauge (0.2-mm) wire. Picking up three or four seed beads at a time on the end of the wire, "stitch" them onto the necklace. You should be able to just push the wire into the necklace with your fingers, but you can thread it onto a needle if you prefer.

This is another piece that was inspired by the jewelry of Ancient Egypt. Armlets incorporating specific stones to protect the wearer were worn by both men and women, and can be seen in many tomb paintings. I've adapted the look to make a modern bangle.

TWO-TONE BANGLE

MATERIALS

0.2-mm fine black pre-knit wire

0.1-mm fine purple pre-knit wire

¾-in. (1.5-cm) square feature bead

32-gauge (0.2-mm) wire

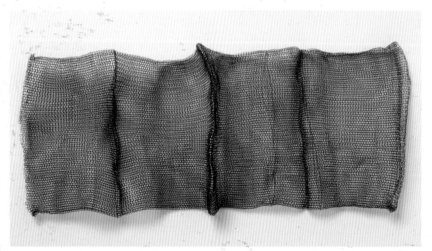

1 Cut a 9-in. (23-cm) length of 0.2-mm fine black pre-knit wire. Fold it in half lengthwise and then in half again, and press with your fingers to make a crease. Unfold the wire.

2 Fold over about ½ in. (1 cm) at one short, raw end and roll it over and over until you reach the first crease mark.

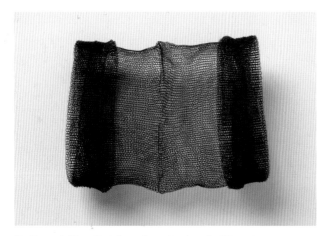

3 Repeat Step 2 at the other short end of the wire.

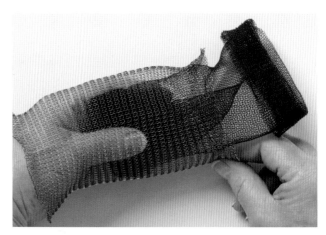

4 Cut a 4½-in. (12.5-cm) length of 0.1-mm fine pre-knit purple wire (or a contrasting color of your choice). Put your hand inside the tube and pull it over the black wire.

5 Tuck the raw ends under the turned-over ends of the black wire.

6 Turn the black ends over twice at each end of the bangle.

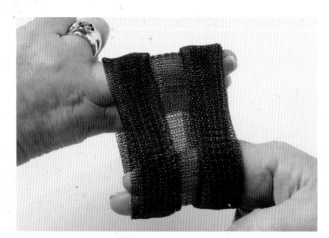

7 Put your hands inside the bangle and push them apart. This helps to mesh the wires together. It also shapes the bangle so that it will fit over your hand.

8 Thread a short length of 32-gauge (0.2-mm) wire through the feature bead and "stitch" it onto the center of the bangle. You should be able to push the wire through the mesh with your fingers, but you can use a needle if you prefer.

MIX-AND-MATCH BANGLES

This look can easily be adapted for daytime wear:
simply match the contrast color of wire to the color
of your outfit.

Geometric shapes were very much a part of the Art Deco and Art Nouveau periods. My shapes were inspired by a visit to Barcelona, where I saw the work of the architect and designer, Antonio Gaudi. Pre-knit wire is easy to manipulate and shape.

GEOMETRIC CUFF

MATERIALS

0.2-mm fine pre-knit gunmetal
bronze wire

Scissors

Fine beading needle

32-gauge (0.2-mm) gunmetal bronze wire

Gunmetal bronze seed beads

6 x 3-mm cube beads in bronze/pink

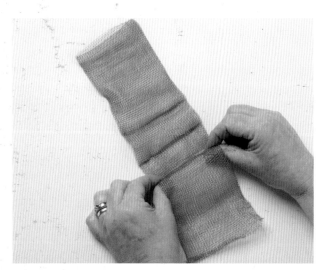

1 Cut a 12-in. (30-cm) length of 0.2-mm fine pre-knit gunmetal bronze wire. Fold it in half lengthwise and crease, then measure 1½ in. (4 cm) out from either side of the crease and crease again, to form guidelines.

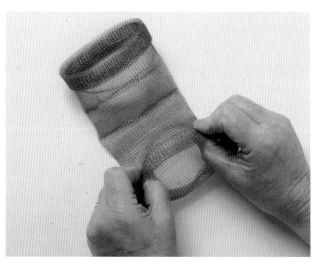

2 Fold over about ½ in. (1 cm) at one short, raw end and roll the wire over and over until you reach the first crease mark. Repeat at the other end of the cuff.

3 Work around the cuff, teasing it into a circular shape with your fingers.

4 Take hold of the central crease with your fingers and pull sharply, so that it stands out above the cuff. You will need to work around the cuff several times until it protrudes to the depth that you want.

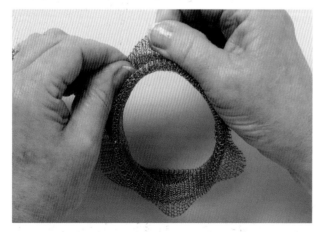

5 Create a fluted edge along the central crease by pulling the wire out with one thumb and pushing it in with the other.

6 Thread a fine beading needle with 32-gauge (0.2-mm) gunmetal bronze wire and stitch seed beads along the edge of the central crease, spacing them evenly.

7 Add a 3-mm cube bead to each raised point on the central fold.

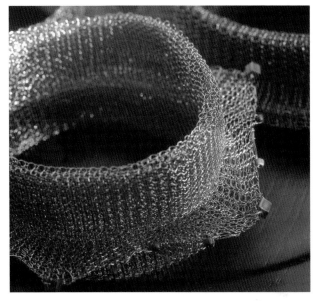

For an elegant, fun evening and prom accessory, the shimmer evening glove fits the bill. This design harks back to the early Victorian era, when no well-bred lady would dream of going outside without wearing gloves. (Indeed, some ladies prided themselves on never going ungloved even while at home!) During the 1840s, crocheted and knitted gloves, were immensely popular, and my design uses pre-knit wire to evoke the elegance of this period.

SHIMMER EVENING GLOVE

MATERIALS

Coarse pre-knit silver wire

Scissors

Large-eyed sewing needle (optional)

10–12 rose beads approx. 5 mm in diameter

Thin fiber knitting yarn

Small crochet hook

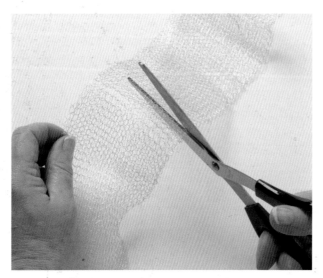

1 Measure from your knuckles to your wrist and add about 2 in. (5 cm) to allow for neatening the ends. Cut a piece of coarse silver pre-knit wire to this length.

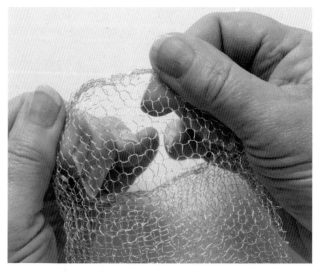

2 Along the wrist edge, roll the wire over a couple of times and press it down with your fingers to get rid of any sharp edges. This also gives a thicker line of silver along the edge, which looks very attractive.

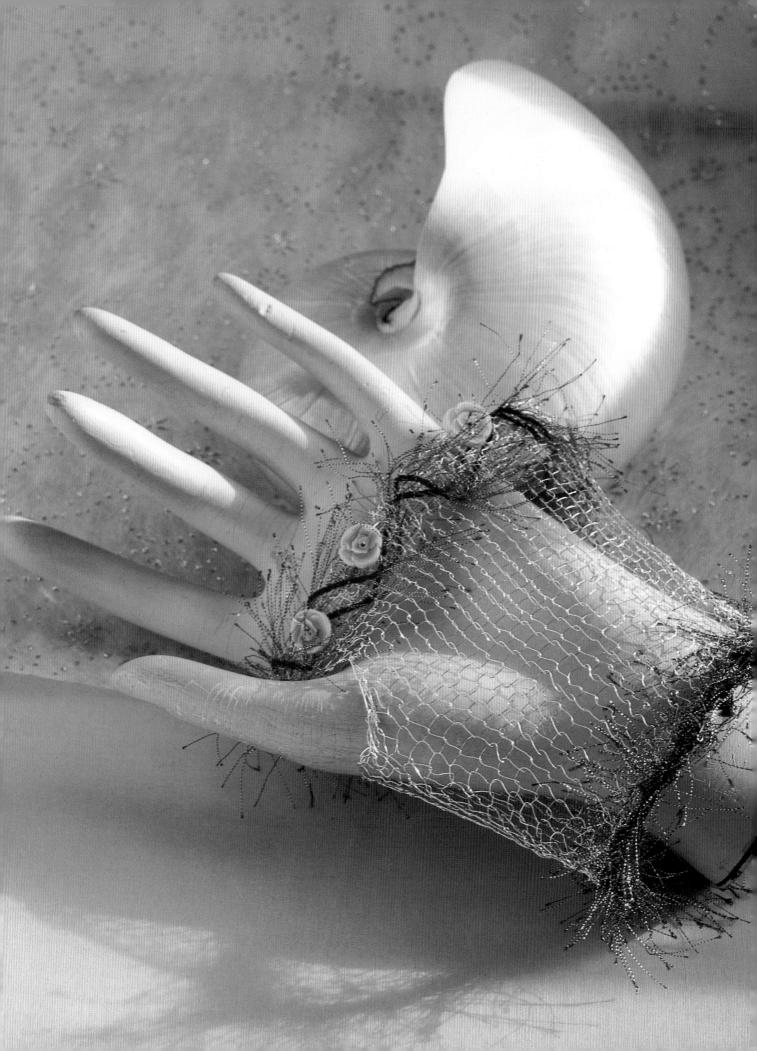

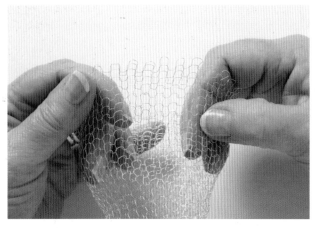

3 At the finger end, tweak the wire so that the rows of pre-knit wire are level, unraveling a row or two if necessary to get a straight edge.

4 Loop the wire that you have unraveled from the mesh around the finger edge to neaten it further. (You can thread the wire onto a large-eyed needle if you find it easier, or simply loop it around with your fingers and pull it taut.) Leave a generous length of wire loose at the end.

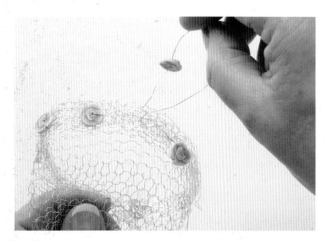

5 Using the loose end of wire from the previous step, attach rose-shaped beads around the wrist edge, as if you're sewing on buttons.

6 Cut a length of fiber yarn the circumference of your wrist plus 1 in. (2.5 cm). Fold over about 1 in. (2.5 cm) of the yarn and lay it along the finger edge of the glove. Holding the folded yarn with your fingers, push a small crochet hook through the pre-knit wire from the front and catch the yarn on the hook. Pull all the yarn through to the front of the glove. Cover the whole edge in this way.

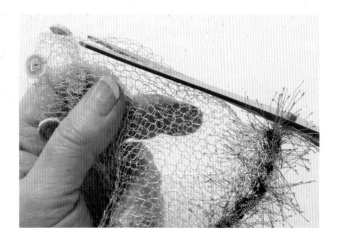

7 Now make the thumb hole. Measure from the base of your thumb to halfway around your thumb and cut a tiny slice out of the glove to this measurement, centering it from top to bottom.

8 Crimp the edge of the thumb hole with your fingers, as in Step 2. Take a piece of unraveled wire and loop it around the thumb hole, as in Step 4, to neaten it.

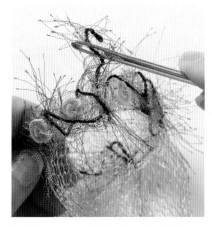

9 Using a crochet hook, attach fiber yarn around the wrist edge, in between the rose beads.

FRUIT-EDGED GLOVE

As a fun and more youthful alternative to the roses, I decorated the edges of these gloves with hand-made beads that look like sections cut through various fruits.

Pre-knit wire comes in so many lovely colors that it's very easy to create a piece to match your outfit. In this design, the pre-knit wire is edged with hand-stitched loops of fine wire and beaded to catch the light.

HAND-STITCHED CHOKER

MATERIALS

Ready-made silver-colored neck piece with removeable ball clasp

0.1-mm fine pre-knit pruple wire

32-gauge (0.2 mm) purple wire

Size 11 glass triangle beads

9–10 4-mm metallic flat-drop beads

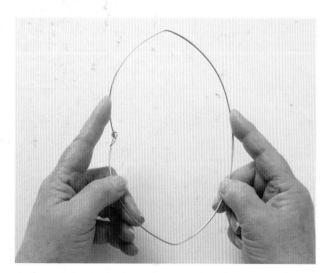

1 Squash the neck piece to an eye-shape by pressing it with your fingers.

2 Cut two pieces of 0.1-mm fine pre-knit purple wire about 4 in. (10 cm) long. You will find that lots of tiny fragments fall off the wire as you cut it, so work over a waste bin.

3 Fold each piece of pre-knit wire in half lengthwise, and press to leave a crease. Open out, then fold each raw edge under by about ¼ in. (0.5 cm), so that it's inside the tube of pre-knit wire, and crimp with your fingers to get a neat edge.

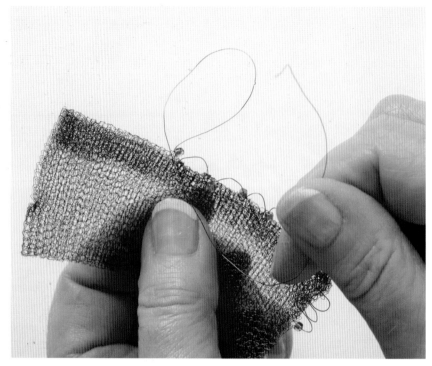

4 Fold the pre-knit wire along the crease line again, making sure that the long sides align. Anchor a length of 32-gauge (0.2-mm) wire on one short side, about ½ in. (1 cm) in from the fold. Pick up one triangle bead and push it down to the end of the wire. Loop the wire through the pre-knit wire from the back and pull it taut to anchor the bead. Push the wire through the mesh from back to front, leaving a small loop along the edge. Holding the loop with your fingers, take the wire back through the mesh and pull it taut to anchor the loop.

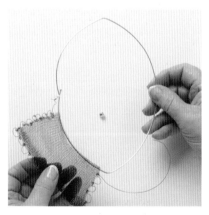

5 Alternating beads and loops, continue working around the raw edges of the pre-knit wire until you are about ½ in. (1 cm) from the folded edge on the opposite short side. Leave about 4 in. (10 cm) of wire loose at the end.

6 Remove the ball clasp from the neck piece, then thread the neck piece through the pre-knit wire along the folded edge.

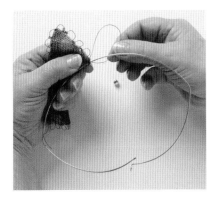

7 Push the pre-knit wire around the neck piece so that one short edge sits in the center, opposite the clasp. Anchor the pre-knit piece on the neck piece by taking the excess wire left at the end of Step 5 around the choker and through the mesh several times. Do not snip off the excess wire, as you will need it in the next step.

8 Using the excess wire, "stitch" four or five flat-drop metallic beads along the short edge that sits in the center of the piece.

9 Repeat Steps 4 through 8 to attach the second piece of pre-knit wire to the neck piece. Re-attach the ball clasp to the end of the choker.

FEATURE-BEAD CHOKER

Make a single feature bead the focus of attention. Finish the piece with simple un-beaded loops along the side and bottom edges.

TWISTED WIRE JEWELRY

WIRE IS SO PLIABLE that, with the exception of the very thickest gauges, you can bend and twist it any way you choose, using only your fingers. You can twist wire around individual beads to create spiky "twigs," wrap one length of beaded wire around another to form interwoven pieces that look incredibly intricate, and bend it into angular shapes of your own choosing. The projects in this chapter are stunningly stylish, yet they have a contemporary feel that makes them suitable for even the trendiest of occasions.

This piece was inspire by the colors of a hydrangea bush in my garden. The wire is twisted around the beads to echo the way many tiny hydrangea florets branch off from one stem.

FLOWER-BUD BRACELET

MATERIALS

24-gauge (0.5-mm) silver wire

Wire cutters

Silver T-bar clasp

Size 10 seed beads—blue assortment

5-mm silver-lined triangle beads

1 Cut about 8 ft (2.4 m) of 24-gauge (0.5-mm) silver wire off the spool. Thread the circular part of the T-bar clasp onto the wire, about halfway along. Twist the wire around the clasp to anchor it.

2 Thread colored seed beads onto one end of the wire.

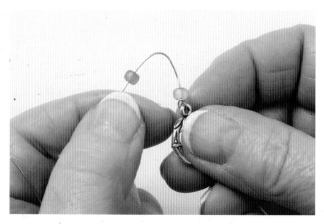

3 Push the first bead up as close to the clasp as possible. Bend the wire into a V-shape about ½ in. (1 cm) long

4 Push the next bead into the point of the V-shape, then twist the wire around several times beneath the bead to anchor it in position.

5 Repeat the process, leaving one bead between each V-shape, until the piece is long enough to fit around your wrist. Leave about 2 in. (5 cm) of wire free at the end.

6 Now take the other end of the wire. Thread on colored seed beads and crystals alternately.

7 Repeat Steps 3 through 5, making twists with the crystals and leaving the blue beads in between the twists.

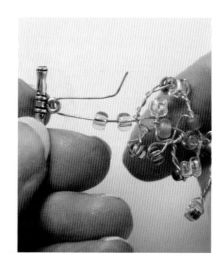

8 Holding the clasp in one hand, twist one wire over the other, adjusting the position of the beaded twists as you go so that the two rows appear to interlock.

9 Thread two or three seed beads that are all the same color onto the loose end of wire that you left in Step 5 and thread on the T-bar part of the clasp, pushing it up against the seed beads. Twist the wire over the clasp to anchor it in place, then wrap the wire in between two of the seed beads to finish. Snip off any excess wire.

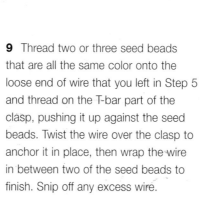

TWIG BRACELETS

Once you've mastered the basic technique, you can adapt this design to suit different outfits or occasions.

The central portion of this necklace—a classy-looking array of beaded twists—hangs from clear elastic bead cord. It looks, at first glance, as if the necklace is simply suspended at the wearer's neck, with no visible means of support.

PEARL NECKLACE

MATERIALS

28-gauge (0.3-mm) champagne-colored wire

Size 6 seed beads—mix of gold, brown, white, and black

0.8-mm clear elastic bead cord

4 x 2-mm gold-colored crimp beads

Gold-plated T-bar clasp

Micro wire crimpers

Flat-nose pliers

1 Cut 6 ft (2 m) of 28-gauge (0.3-mm) champagne-colored wire. Fold the wire in half and twist the loose ends together. Thread seed beads onto the wire.

2 Push two beads along to the end of the wire. About ¼ in. (0.5 cm) from the end of the wire, bend the wire into a V-shape about ½ in. (1 cm) long. Push the next bead into the point of the V-shape, then twist the wire around several times beneath the bead to anchor it in position. Continue making beaded twists, leaving two beads between each twist and varying the lengths of the twists a little.

3 Continue doing this until the twisted and beaded wire is approximately 12 in. (30 cm) long.

4 Hold the loose ends of the wire in one hand and fold the twisted and beaded wire in half. Insert your finger into the loop and carefully and loosely twist the two sides together.

5 Twist the loose ends of wire together and form them into a loop, leaving a short tail. Wrap the tail of wire several times around the last bead to secure it. Press with your flat-nose pliers and snip off any excess

6 Work out how long you want the clear elastic bead cord to be and add 4 in. (10 cm). Tie the cord in a double knot around the center of the beaded section.

7 Working from the center outward, wrap the loose ends of the cord around the beaded section. You should end up with the same amount of cord protruding at each end. Trim if necessary to make them the same length.

8 At each end, twist the cord around the last bead.

9 Thread two crimp beads onto one end of the cord, followed by one half of the clasp.

10 Push the protruding end of the cord back through the crimp beads.

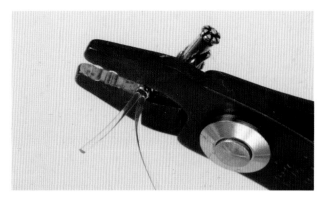

11 Crimp the beads with micro wire crimpers to secure. Attach the other half of the clasp to the other end of the cord in the same way.

AMBER GLOW NECKLACE

For a lighter-looking alternative, use pearl and amber-colored beads. This would look wonderful worn with a low-cut ball gown.

In this bracelet, a frame is made from zigzags of wire that are then filled in with beads of your choice. I've listed the types of beads that I used in the materials list—but you can vary the quantities and types to suit your own taste.

ZIGZAG BRACELET

MATERIALS

16-gauge (1.2-mm) silver wire

28-gauge (0.3-mm) silver wire

7-mm silver-lined cane beads

7-mm crystal bead

Size 5 silver-lined triangle beads

Medium black cane beads

Size 11 rainbow triangle beads

5-mm black fancy beads mix

2-mm black metallic beads

Silver toggle clasp

Wire cutter

Round-nose pliers

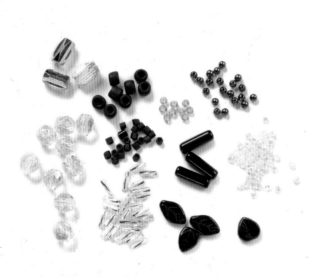

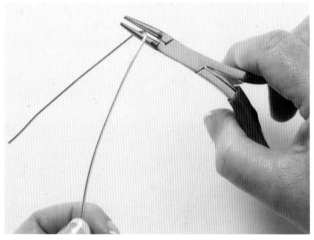

1 Cut 2 ft (60 cm) of 16-gauge (1.2-mm) silver wire. Using round-nose pliers, bend the wire into a V-shape about 2½ in. (6 cm) from the end. Form another V-shaped bend 2 in. (5 cm) from the first.

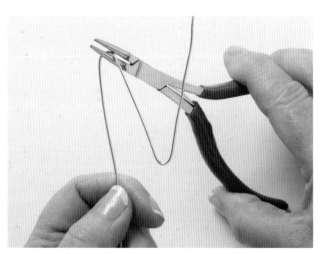

2 Bend the rest of the wire into V-shapes at 2-in. (5-cm) intervals to create a zigzag pattern, until the bracelet sits comfortably around your wrist (on average, four complete V-shapes). Cut off any excess wire.

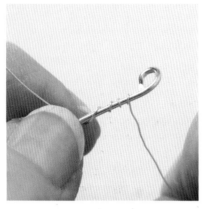

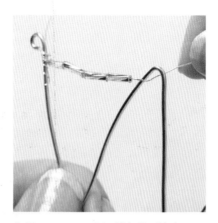

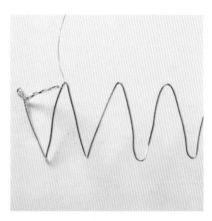

3 Take the end of the wire in the tip of your round-nose pliers and curl it inward toward the first V. Repeat at the other end of the wire, again curling it inward. Working from the spool, wrap 28-gauge (0.3-mm) silver wire around the bracelet, just under the curl.

4 Now you need to fill in the V-shapes to make triangles. Thread four 7-mm silver-lined cane beads onto the thinner wire, then take the wire across the top of the first V-shape to the tip of the next one. Wrap the wire around the tip of the second V several times to secure it, then cut it off the spool.

5 Repeat Step 4 at the other end of the bracelet, but do not cut the wire off the spool.

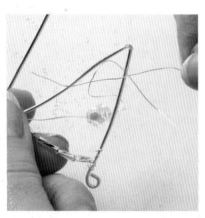

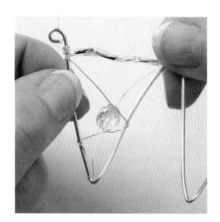

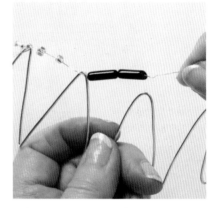

6 Thread a 7-mm crystal onto the wire. When the bead is in the center of the V, form a loop in the wire. Feed the end of the wire through the loop, around the larger wire frame, and pull taut to anchor the crystal in place.

7 Criss-cross the thinner wire randomly over this triangle, wrapping it around the wire frame.

8 Thread two size-5 silver-lined triangle beads onto the wire, then take the wire across to the tip of the next V. Wrap the wire around the tip of the second V several times to secure it, but do not cut it off the spool. Repeat the process in the next V, using two medium black cane beads.

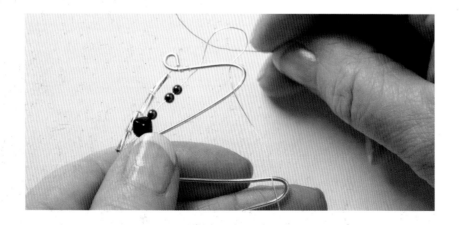

9 Complete the next triangle using twelve size 11 rainbow triangle beads. Then fill in the final triangle with one 5-mm fancy bead and three 2-mm black metallic beads, criss-crossing the wire around the frame as in Step 7.

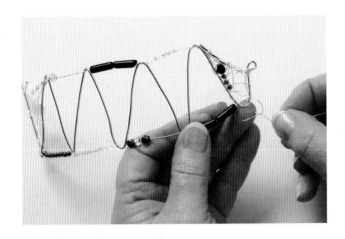

10 Turn the bracelet upside down and fill in the triangles along the base in the same way, using whatever beads you like from those listed. I used nine 2-mm metallic black beads in the first triangle, twelve size 11 rainbow beads in the second triangle, two 5-mm black fancy beads and a glass triangle in the third, and two medium black cane beads in the fourth. Fasten off the wire on the last triangle, as shown.

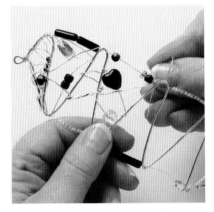

11 Cut a new piece of 28-gauge (0.3-mm) silver wire and fill in the centers of the triangles as in Step 9, using any beads you like from those listed. Keep some beads loose and some tightly anchored with a web of criss-crossing wire.

BEADED TIARA

This tiara is made in exactly the same way as the bracelet. Only the shape of the outer frame is different.

12 Attach a toggle clasp (see page 20) to complete the bracelet.

Dew drops in the early morning or raindrops after a summer shower made me think of crystal chandelier earrings for fairies and other wee garden folk. Make the wire frames at the same time, so that they look indentical.

CRYSTAL CHANDELIER EARRINGS

MATERIALS

Spool of 32-gauge (0.2-mm) silver wire

20 4-mm Czech pale pink crystals

60 3-mm Czech clear crystals

Ready-made diamond earring shapes

Spring-loaded silver pierced earwires

Wire cutters

Round- and flat-nose pliers

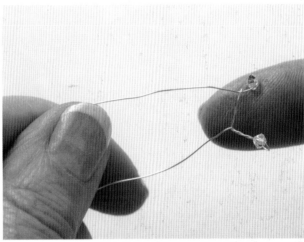

1 Cut a 9–10-in. (22–25-cm) length of 32-gauge (0.2-mm) silver wire and thread on two 3-mm clear crystals. About 4 in. (10 cm) from the end of the wire, twist the wire two or three times around the first crystal. About ½ in. (1 cm) further along the wire, twist the wire around the second crystal in the same way, so that the two twists form a V-shape.

2 Thread on one 4-mm pink crystal and two 3-mm clear crystals. Allow the pink crystal to sit at the top of the V-shape.

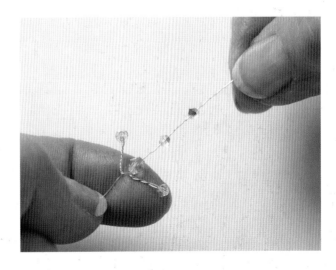

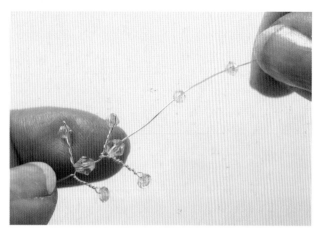

3 Twist the wire around the next pair of smaller crystals, as in Step 1.

4 Repeat Steps 2 and 3.

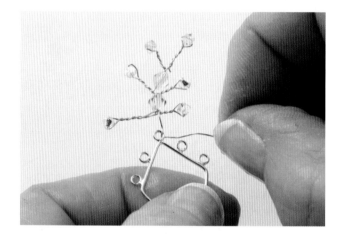

5 Repeat Steps 1 through 4 to make ten units in total (five for each earring), varying the lengths of wire so that the crystals will hang at different heights.

6 Insert the excess wire of the first "branch" into the diamond earring shape to begin forming a chandelier.

7 Wrap the protruding wire around the frame of the diamond earring shape, press firmly with your flat-nose pliers, and snip off any excess.

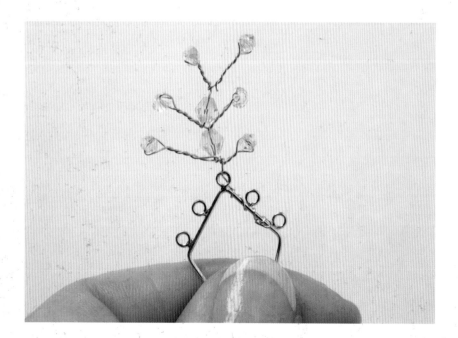

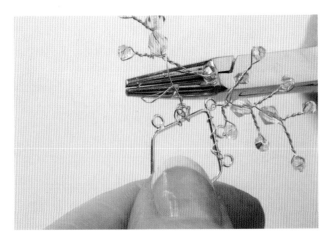

8 Attach the remaining four units to the frame, staggering the lengths so that the crystals hang at different heights. Twist the protruding wires around themselves, rather than around the frame.

9 Using the tips of your round-nose pliers, open up the loop at the base of the earwire. Insert the "chandelier" and close up the loop again.

PRECIOUS PEARL EARRINGS

By using pearls instead of crystals, you can create earrings that provide all-day glamour!

When even your hair needs to glimmer and sparkle on a magical evening, a jeweled hair comb is perfect for creating style. Hair combs were often worn as part of antique and vintage jewelry sets.

VINTAGE JEWELED HAIR COMB

MATERIALS

65 x 5-mm round pearl beads

28-gauge (0.3-mm) gold-colored wire

Hair comb

10–15 silver-lined gold hex beads, size 8

9–12 6-x-4-mm brown cone crystals

Bead mat

Wire cutters

Flat-nose pliers

1 Working from the spool, thread about 65 5-mm round pearl beads onto 28-gauge (0.3-mm) gold-colored wire.

2 With the front of the comb facing you, and leaving about 4 in. (10 cm) from the end of the wire, take the wire up between the edge of the comb and the first tooth. Take up enough beads to fill the width of the comb, then take the wire down between the last tooth and the edge of the comb.

3 Wrap the wire over the front of the comb, and take it back down between the last and penultimate teeth.

4 Take up one pearl bead, bend the wire into a "V" about ½ in. (1 cm) above the comb, leaving the bead in the "V." Twist the wire around two or three times just under the bead, to fix it in place.

5 Work along the comb, forming a beaded twist between alternate teeth. Vary the heights of the twists a little as you go, and work the twists from the back of the comb each time.

6 Work a second row of beaded twists in the same way, this time working the twists from the front of the comb so that the rows are nicely separated from one another. Work a third row, again varying the heights of the twists. Snip the wire off the spool, leaving about 4 in. (10 cm) at the end.

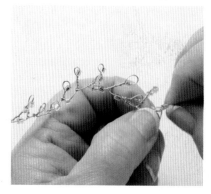

7 Working from the spool, thread 10–15 silver-lined gold hex beads onto the wire. Make beaded twists, as before, incorporating one or two beads into each twist and leaving one or two beads in between each twist. Continue until you have a length of beaded twists about 4 in. (10 cm) long. Snip the wire off the spool, leaving a short tail at the end.

8 Working from the front of the comb, insert the loose tail of wire between the edge of the comb and the first tooth, and hold it securely on the back of the comb. Wind the length of wire twists in and out of the rows of pearl twists, adjusting the position with your fingers as you go.

9 Bring the wire up through the last tooth and cut, leaving a short tail. Cut about 36 in. (90 cm) of wire. Thread on three crystals. Insert one end of the wire into the comb from the front, and hold it securely on the back of the comb. Make a small loop in the wire, hold two crystals at the top of the loop, and allow the third crystal to fall halfway down between the top of the loop and the comb.

WEDDING COMB

Made using pearls in soft pastel shades, this comb would enhance a bridal outfit at a summer wedding.

BARRETTES AND HAIR GRIPS

All sorts of hair accessories can be decorated in exactly the same way. Select the type and color of bead to suit the occasion.

10 Immediately above the bead that you've allowed to drop, twist the wire around the bead, trapping it in position on the wire stem. Repeat Steps 9 and 10 three or four times across the width of the comb, making sure that you space the crystal twists evenly.

11 Weave the excess wires in and out of the teeth of the comb, making sure they come out on the front. It's important not to have any sharp, loose ends on the back of the comb, as they might scratch your head when you wear it.

12 Wrap each protruding wire around the nearest beaded twist several times to secure it. Press the end firmly with your flat-nose pliers, and cut off any excess.

In this bracelet, four separate strands of pearl and crystal beads are wrapped around each other to form a chunky, interwoven mass. This bracelet would look stunning worn with a classic little black dress.

INTERWOVEN TREASURES BRACELET

MATERIALS

Collapsible-eye needle

Black beading twine

17 10-mm grey-black beads

Swarovski 4-mm black pearl beads

8 4-mm gray crystal beads tinged with gold

Toho size 11 matt black beads

Toho size 11 silver-lined black beads

20 gray freshwater pearl "potatoes"

3 10-mm gray pearls

24-gauge (0.5-mm) champagne-colored wire

Size 7 steel (1.5-mm) crochet hook

28-gauge (0.3-mm) champagne-colored wire

Wire cutters

Gold plated T-bar clasp

1 Cut two 24-in. (60-cm) lengths of black beading twine and thread them into a collapsible-eye needle. Thread on 17 large gray-black beads.

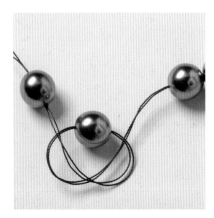

2 Tie a knot in the twine between each bead.

3 Cut a length of 24-gauge (0.5-mm) champagne-colored wire three times the length that you want the finished bracelet to be. Thread on groups of four 4-mm black pearl beads and one crystal, until you have covered about half to two-thirds of the wire.

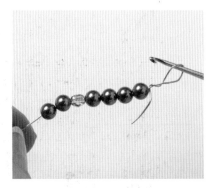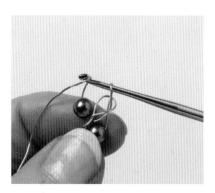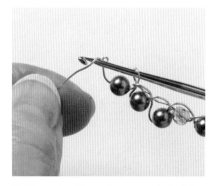

4 Wrap the end of the wire around a 7 steel (1.5-mm) crochet hook to form a loop, then twist the end of the wire around several times to hold the loop in place.

5 Take up one bead, then work a crochet slip stitch (see page 22).

6 Repeat until you have crocheted the entire length of the wire. (You may find that you need to add on more beads.)

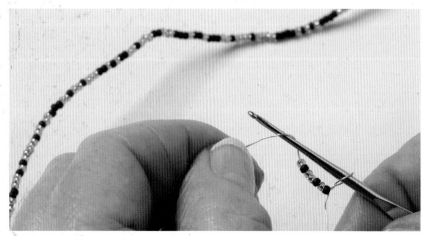

7 Cut 3 ft (90 cm) of 28-gauge (0.3-mm) champagne-colored wire. Thread on a mix of the two colors of Toho beads until you have covered about 2 ft (60 cm) of the wire. Using a 7 steel (1.5mm) crochet hook, form a loop, then twist the end of the wire around several times to hold the loop in place. Take up six or seven beads, then work a crochet slip stitch (see page 22).

8 Continue until you have crocheted the entire length of the wire.

9 Take the pearl and crystal wire and wrap it around the large, gray-black bead chain.

10 Repeat with the Toho beads chain.

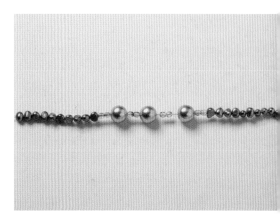

11 Cut about 3 ft (90 cm) of 24-gauge (0.5mm) gold-colored wire. Thread on potato pearls, gray crystals, and three large gray pearls in the sequence shown above.

12 Center the three large pearls on the top of the bracelet, then wrap the remainder of the wire around the bracelet, as before, leaving a short length of wire at each end for the clasp.

13 Attach a T-bar clasp to complete the bracelet (see page 20).

VARIATION

For a fresher, lighter look, replace the dark, brooding blacks and grays with white pearls, tiny crystals, and just four or five large, copper-colored beads.

CHAPTER 4

COILED WIRE JEWELRY

THE PROJECTS in this chapter were created by wrapping wire around a mandrel or other circular or conical object. You can make same-sized coils or gently tapering spirals. Wire holds it shape well—but if you find that your piece of jewelry has become a little distorted with wear, simply press it back into shape again with your fingers.

Driving through any part of England's countryside in high summer treats your eyes to a veritable delight of mouth-watering greens in every tone and hue. Such landscapes what inspired these earrings.

MEADOW-GREEN TWIRL EARRINGS

MATERIALS

19-gauge (0.9-mm) silver-plated wire

Assortment of size 8 green seed beads

Silver earwires

Wire cutters

Mandrel or dowel

Round-nose pliers

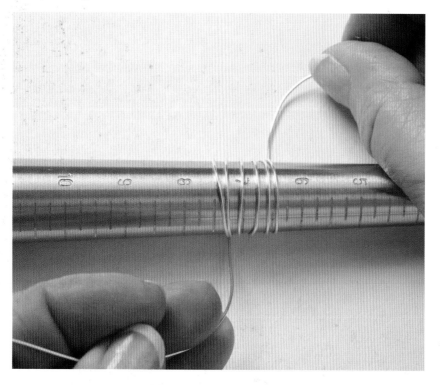

1 Work out how long you want the finished earrings to be, then cut twice this amount of 19-gauge (0.9-mm) silver-plated wire. Hold the wire along the side of a mandrel or dowel and wrap it nine or ten times around your chosen diameter, pushing the coils upward as you work so that you're wrapping the wire around the same point every time.

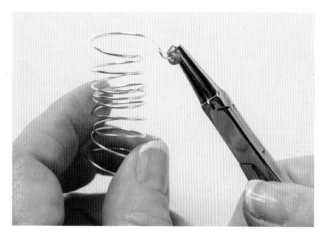

2 Feed a glass bead onto the end of the wire and, using the tips of your round-nose pliers, curl the end of the wire into a loop to secure the bead.

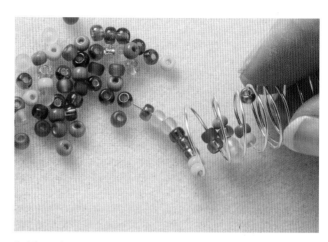

3 Thread more beads onto the other end of the wire. You can put on as many or as few as you wish; I like a very full effect, so I put about 30 beads on each earring.

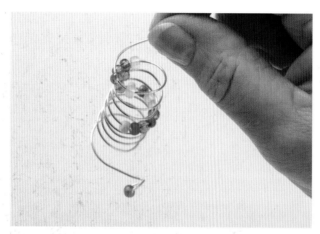

4 Shake the coil so that the beads travel down the wire. This enables you to see whether or not you've got the fullness of beads that you want.

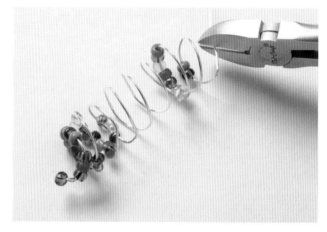

5 Twist the last coil so that it aligns with the loop that you made at the end of the wire in Step 2. Snip off any excess wire just beyond this point.

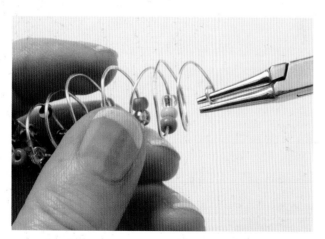

6 Using the tips of your round-nose pliers, form a complete loop at the top of the earring, at the very end of the wire.

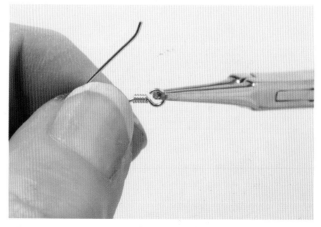

7 Using the tips of your round-nose pliers, open the loop on the earwire.

8 Feed the beaded coil onto the earwire.

9 Using the tips of your round-nose pliers, close the loop again. Squeeze the ends of the loop past one another; they'll spring apart slightly when you release the pliers.

10 If necessary, insert your fingers into the coil to reshape it, as it may have become slightly misshapen as you work.

SUNSHINE EARRINGS

For this version, I chose colors from a summer border in my garden—hot oranges and yellows to remind me of sunny days!

Horses on fairground carousels, going up and down and round and round at the same time, produce flashes of light and dashes of colors from their highly ornate leatherware and painted tin bodies. As a little girl, my favorite carousel horse was called Mr Spangles. The movement of color that this bracelet creates reminds me of him—hence the name, Spangles Bangle.

SPANGLES BANGLE

MATERIALS

16-gauge (1.2-mm) silver-plated wire

32-gauge (0.2-mm) silver-plated wire

Double delicia beads—mixed colors

Mandrel

Wire cutters

Round- and flat-nose pliers

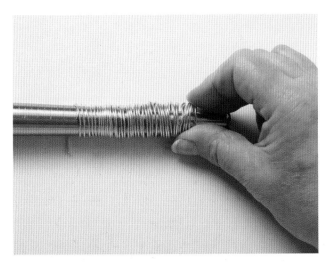

1 Coil 16-gauge (1.2-mm) silver-plated wire around the mandrel about 50 times, pushing the coils upward as you work so that you're wrapping the wire around the same point every time, then cut it off the spool.

2 Remove the coiled wire from the mandrel. Using the tips of your round-nose pliers, curl a small loop at the end of the wire. Grip the curl tightly in your flat-nose pliers, then curl the wire around to form a tight spiral about ½ in. (1 cm) across. Repeat at the other end of the coiled wire.

3 Bend the spirals at 90° to the coiled wire. Push the coiled wire to squash the coils together, so that they're almost flat and overlapping each other, rather like a stack of dominoes that has fallen over.

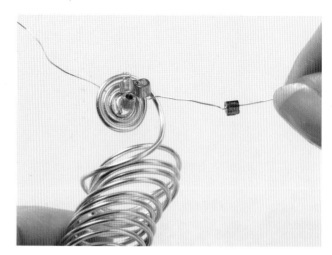

4 Take a short length of 32-gauge (0.2-mm) silver-plated wire. Insert it into one of the spiral, leaving the end loose. Take up a double delica bead and push it down onto the spiral.

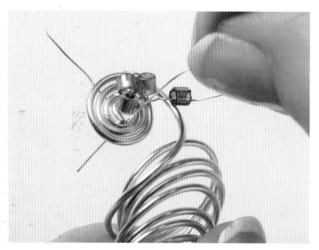

5 "Overstitch" the bead onto the spiral, using the wire like sewing thread. Continue until you have virtually filled the spiral with beads.

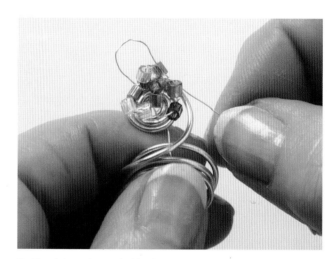

6 Bead the other spiral in the same way.

7 Weave the loose ends in and out of the spiral several times. Finish off by pushing the end of the wire through a bead, pulling it really tight, and snipping off the excess.

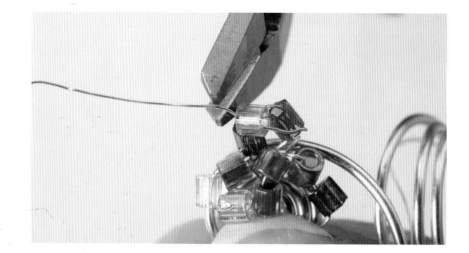

ROUND-COIL BRACELET

To create a softer effect and work with
an alternative color scheme, use this
champagne-colored wire. Press the wire just
gently in Step 3, so that the coil shapes
remain more rounded and upright.

Nature never seems to clash her colors, and looking at a herbaceous border in high summer always inspires me to sketch shapes and color combinations. The colors in this bracelet were inspired by the large border at Culzean Castle in Ayrshire, Scotland.

LEMON-DROP BRACELET

MATERIALS

16-gauge (1.2-mm) gunmetal bronze wire

32-gauge (0.2-mm) gunmetal bronze wire

32-gauge (0.2-mm) wire in contrasting color

Selection of beads in toning colors,
in different shapes and sizes

Antique bronze-finish T-clasp

Wire cutters

Flat-nose pliers

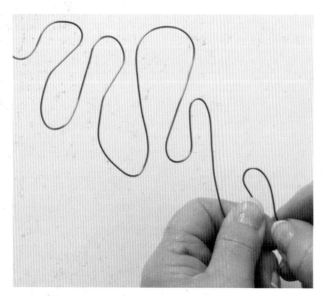

1 Cut about 24 in. (60 cm) of 16-gauge (1.2-mm) gunmetal bronze wire. Using your fingers, bend it into a series of irregularly shaped squiggles.

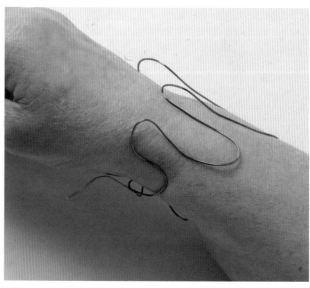

2 Check that the bent wire fits around your wrist and adjust it if necessary. Cut off any excess wire.

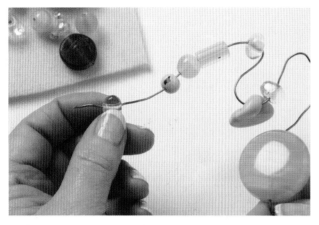

3 Thread the beads onto the bent wire, placing your large focal bead in the center. Adjust the bends in the wire at this point if you wish; once the beads are in position, you may decide you want the bends to be in different places.

4 Feed the circular part of the T-clasp onto the wire, leaving about 1 in. (2.5 cm) protruding. Bend the excess wire over the clasp, wrap it around to secure, and press the ends flat with your flat-nose pliers so that there are no sharp ends sticking out.

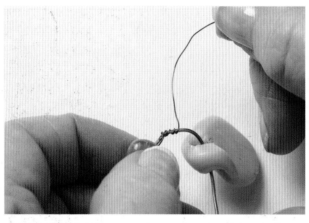

5 Take a spool of 32-gauge (0.2mm) wire in a contrasting color, feed the end into the second last bead, then wrap the wire around the thicker, bent wire.

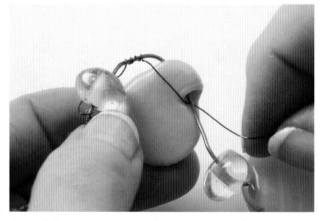

6 When you get to a bead, take the wire across the back of the bead, then continue wrapping the thinner wire around the thicker one, as before.

7 Repeat the wrapping process. This prevents the beads from slipping on the wire and also creates texture.

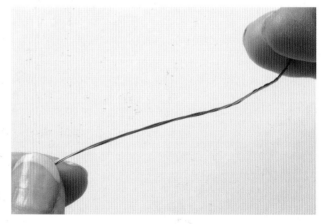

8 Cut a 6-ft (2-m) length of 32-gauge (0.2mm) gunmetal bronze wire. Fold it in half, and then in half again, and twist it in your fingers.

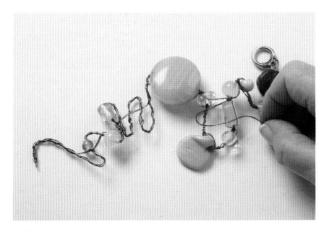

9 Wrap the twisted wire around the end of the bracelet several times to anchor it. Take the twisted wire across the loops of the bent, thick wire, wrapping it around the bracelet to fix it in place.

10 Feed the T-bar of the clasp onto the other end of the bracelet, leaving about 1 in. (2.5 cm) of wire protruding. Bend the excess wire over the clasp, wrap it around to secure, and press the ends flat with your flat-nose pliers so that there are no sharp ends sticking out.

SOFT-CENTERED BRACELETS

Here, in addition to varying the color of the wire and beads, I wrapped some fluffy knitting yarn around the wires to create a contrast in texture.

This design was inspired by my love of Greece and one of my favorite places, Sami, on Cephalonia—the island made famous by Louis de Bernières' novel, Captain Corelli's Mandolin. Sitting by the harbor at twilight after dinner, I watched the rays of the setting sun bounce off the mountains and reflect a beautiful light over the sea. I have tried to recreate the same soft, pearly-gray light in this ring, using a mix of gray and pewter double delica beads.

CEPHALONIAN TWILIGHT RING

MATERIALS

Spool of 21-gauge (0.7-mm) silver wire

Spool of 28-gauge (0.3-mm) silver-plated wire

Double delica beads—gray and pewter shimmer

Mandrel

Round-nose pliers

Wire cutters

1 Cut about 15 in. (38 cm) of 21-gauge (0.7-mm) silver wire and wrap it around the mandrel four times. Push the coils upward as you work, so that you're wrapping the wire around the same point every time and all the coils are the same size. This makes the shank of the ring.

2 Holding the coils together, slide the ring shank up to the top of the mandrel and wind the wire three times around the very smallest part of the mandrel.

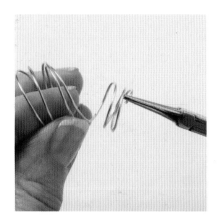

3 Using the tips of your round-nose pliers, make a small curl at each end of the wire.

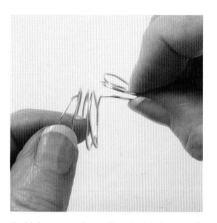

4 Using your fingertips, twist the small coils through 90° so that they sit at right angles to the ring shank.

5 Push the small coils across so that they sit on top of the ring shank, with the cut end over the cut end of the shank.

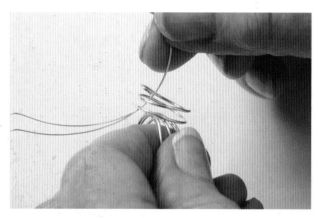

6 Cut 18 in. (45 cm) of 28-gauge (0.3-mm) silver-plated wire and fold it in half. Holding the ring shank in one hand, take the folded loop of the fine wire up to the top of the small circle, feeding it between the ring shank and the edge of the small circle.

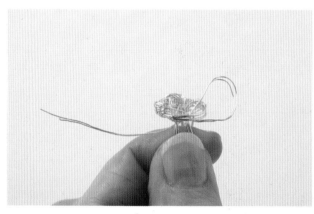

7 Take the wire over the edge of the small circle, down into the center of the ring, and back out through the shank on the other side. Turn the ring and repeat to complete a figure-of-eight motion. Repeat several times, creating a tight mesh on the top of the circle to hold it in position.

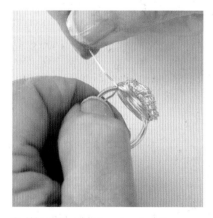

8 Wrap the wire three or four times around the base of the top of the ring. Bring the loose end up into the top of the ring and curl it around the mesh to secure.

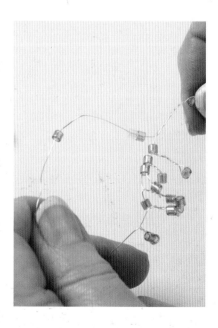

9 Cut 18 in. (45 cm) of 28-gauge (0.3-mm) silver-plated wire and thread it with 20–25 gray and pewter-effect double delica beads. Starting about 4 in. (10 cm) from the end, bend the wire, leaving one bead sitting in the "V" of the bend, and then twist the two strands of wire together immediately below the bead to fix it in place. Continue making twists about 1.5 cm (¾ in.) long, leaving one bead between each twist, until you have twisted up about 3 in. (7.5 cm) of wire.

10 Cross the loose ends over one another to form a tight circle and position them on the top of the ring.

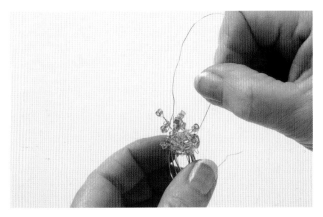

11 Using the loose ends, bind the twisted bead coil onto the top of the ring, using the same figure-of-eight motion shown in Step 7.

COPPER-COIL RING AND PEARL-TOPPED RING

Changing the color scheme creates a totally different feel. Copper wire and iridescent blue-black beads (left) make a bold, dramatic statement, while tiny round pearls (right) look delicate and almost ethereal.

The shape of this cuff is very much influenced by the Ancient Egyptian era, while the colors were taken from the iridescent blues and blacks of ravens' wings shimmering in the sunlight.

RAVEN'S WING CUFF

MATERIALS

19-gauge (0.9-mm) silver-plated wire

19-gauge (0.9-mm) black wire

28-gauge (0.3-mm) silver-plated wire

Selection of black, pewter, gray, glass, and metallic beads in different shapes and sizes

Wire cutters

Round-nose pliers

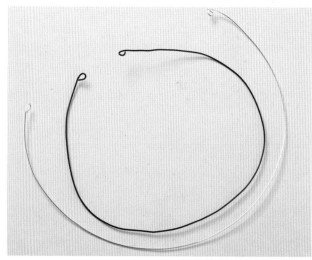

1 Cut a 12-in. (30-cm) length of 19-gauge (0.9-mm) silver-plated and a 12-in. (30-cm) length of 19-gauge (0.9mm) black wire. Using the tips of your round-nose pliers, coil each end of each wire inward to form a small loop.

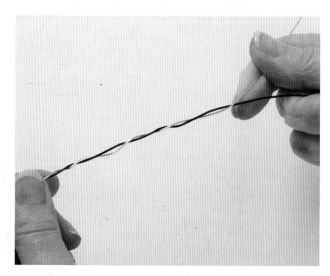

2 Using your fingers, twist the two wires loosely together.

3 Overlap the ends by about 2 in. (5 cm).

4 Undo the loops that you made in Step 1 and wind the wires around the twisted wire.

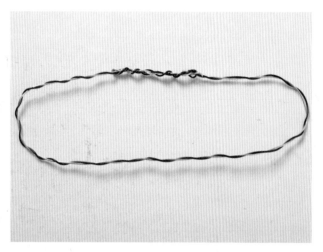

5 Using your fingers, shape the piece into a rough rectangle.

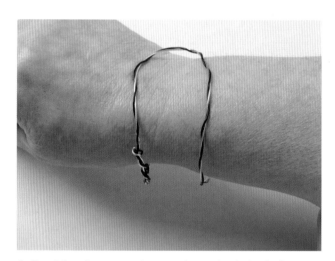

6 Bend the piece around your wrist to check the fit. (It should not go completely around your wrist.)

7 Cut a piece of 28-gauge (0.3-mm) silver-plated wire about twice as long as the circumference of the twisted wire frame, and thread on your selection of beads until you have covered about two-thirds of the wire. Tie a knot about 6 in. (15 cm) from each end.

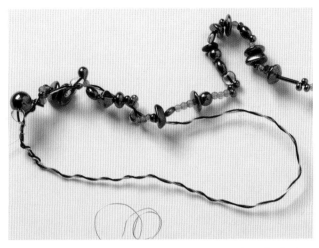

8 Starting at the join in the frame and leaving the tail of wire protruding, wrap the string of beads around the frame.

9 When you get back around to the join, wrap the tails of wire twice around the frame, then hide them between two beads and snip off any excess, making sure there are no sharp ends protruding.

WOODLAND CUFF

The colors on this cuff were taken from photographs of woodland floors in fall, when every shade of brown and gold dances before your eyes.

WIRE CONVERSION CHART

Depending on where you buy your wire, different measurements are used to denote the thickness of the wire. The chart below will enable you to convert quickly from one system to another.

SWG — Imperial Standard Wire Gauge	Wire Number	AWG — American Wire Gauge	AWG — Metric
Inches	Gauge	Inches	Millimetres
0.5000	0000000 (7/0)		
0.4400	000000 (6/0)	0.58000	14.7320
0.4320	00000 (5/0)	0.51650	13.1191
0.4000	0000 (4/0)	0.46000	11.6840
0.3720	000 (3/0)	0.40964	10.4040
0.3480	00 (2/0)	0.36480	9.2660
0.3240	0 (1/0)	0.32486	8.2520
0.3000	1	0.28930	7.3480
0.2760	2	0.25763	6.5430
0.2520	3	0.22942	5.8270
0.2320	4	0.20430	5.1890
0.2120	5	0.18190	4.6210
0.1920	6	0.16200	4.1150
0.1760	7	0.14430	3.6650
0.1600	8	0.12850	3.2640
0.1440	9	0.11440	2.9060
0.1280	10	0.10190	2.5880
0.1160	11	0.09070	2.3040
0.1040	12	0.08080	2.0520
0.0920	13	0.07200	1.8290
0.0800	14	0.06410	1.6280
0.0720	15	0.05710	1.4500
0.0640	16	0.05080	1.2910
0.0560	17	0.04530	1.1500
0.0480	18	0.04030	1.0240
0.0400	19	0.03590	0.9119
0.0360	20	0.03200	0.8128
0.0320	21	0.02850	0.7239
0.0280	22	0.02530	0.6426
0.0240	23	0.02260	0.5740
0.0220	24	0.02010	0.5106
0.0200	25	0.01790	0.4547

SWG — Imperial Standard Wire Gauge	Wire Number	AWG — American Wire Gauge	AWG — Metric
Inches	Gauge	Inches	Millimetres
0.0180	26	0.01590	0.4038
0.0164	27	0.01420	0.3606
0.0148	28	0.01260	0.3200
0.0136	29	0.01130	0.2870
0.0124	30	0.01000	0.2540
0.0116	31	0.00890	0.2261
0.0108	32	0.00800	0.2032
0.0100	33	0.00710	0.1803
0.0092	34	0.00630	0.1601
0.0084	35	0.00560	0.1422
0.0076	36	0.00500	0.1270
0.0068	37	0.00450	0.1143
0.0060	38	0.00400	0.1016
0.0052	39	0.00350	0.0889
0.0048	40	0.00310	0.0787
0.0044	41	0.00280	0.0711
0.0040	42	0.00250	0.0635
0.0036	43	0.00220	0.0559
0.0032	44	0.00200	0.0508
0.0028	45	0.00180	0.0457
0.0024	46	0.00160	0.0406
0.0020	47	0.00140	0.0350
0.0016	48	0.00120	0.0305
0.0012	49	0.00110	0.0279
0.0010	50	0.00100	0.0254
	51	0.00088	.0224
	52	0.00078	0.0198
	53	0.00070	0.0178
	54	0.00062	0.0158
	55	0.00055	0.0140
	56	0.00049	0.0124

SUPPLIERS

This directory lists the bead suppliers that I have chosen to use, but there are many more for you to discover for yourself. Using an internet search engine to look for bead suppliers, you can find dozens of great sources of beads and wire. Do not forget that if beads are purchased from abroad, you may be charged import duty and tax. It is often easier to check whether you can obtain the beads you need from a local bead importer before ordering them from abroad.

UK Suppliers

African Trade Beads
African beads and beading supplies
www.africantradebeads.com

Bead Addict
beads and beading supplies
www.beadaddict.co.uk

Bead Aura
3 Neals Yard
London WC2H 9DP
020 7836 3002
beads and beading supplies
beadaura@gmail.com
www.beadaura.co.uk

The Bead Merchant
P. O. Box 5025
Coggeshall
Essex CO6 1HW
Tel: 0870 609 3035
Fax 0870609 3036
www.beadmerchant.co.uk/

Beads Direct Limited
3 Birch Lea
East Leake
Loughborough
Liecs LE12 6LA
01509 852 187
Service@beadsdirect.co.uk
www.beadsdirect.co.uk

Bead Shop
21A Tower Street
London WC2 9NS
020 7240 0931
beads and beading supplies
www.beadshop.co.uk

Beads Unllimited
P. O. Box 1
Hove BN3 3SG
01273 740 777
www.beadsunlimited.co.uk

Beadworks
online retailer of beads and beading supplies
www.beadworks.co.uk

Bijoux Beads
Elton House
2 Abbey Street
Bath BA1 1NN
01225 482024
beads and beading supplies
www.bijouxbeads.co.uk

Crystals
20 shops across southern England selling crystals and beading supplies
www.crystalshop.co.uk

London Bead Company
339 Kentish Town Road
London NW5 2TJ
0870 203 2323
beads and beading supplies
www.londonbeadco.co.uk

Spangles 4 Beads
beads and beading supplies
www.spangles4beads.co.uk

The Viking Loom
22 High Petergate
York YO1 7EH
01904 765559
enquiries@vikingloom.co.uk
www.vikingloom.co.uk

Scientific Wire Company
18 Raven Road
South Woodford
London E18 1HW
020 8505 0002
dan@wires.co.uk
www.scientificwire.com

US Suppliers

Beadalon
205 Carter Drive
West Chester, PA 19382
866-423-2325
*beading wire, stringing materials,
tools*
www.beadalon.com

The Beadin' Path
15 Main Street
Freeport, ME 04032
877-922-3237
vintage Lucite, unique beads/findings

Blue Moon Beads/Westrim Crafts
7855 Hayvenhurst Aveune
Van Nuys, CA 91406
800-377-6715
beads/findings
www.bluemoonbeads.com

Caravan Beads, Inc.
915 Forest Ave
Portland ME 04103
Orders: 800-203-8941
Other: 207-761-2503
Fax: 207-874-2664
www.caravanbeads.com

Ann Dillon
*online retailer of beads and beading
supplies*
www.anndillon.com

Euro Tool, Inc.
14101 Botts Road
Grandview, MO 64030
800-552-3131
tools, beading accessories
www.eurotool.com

Fire Mountain Gems and Beads
1 Fire Mountain Way
Grants Pass, OR 97526
800-355-2137
*beads/findings, tools, stringing
materials, kits*
www.firemountaingems.com

Great Craft Works
133 West Gay Street
West Chester, PA 19380
888-811-5773
beads, tools, stringing materials
www.greatcraftworks.com

Halcraft, USA
30 West 24th Street
New York, NY 10010
212-376-1580
beads, tiny glass marbles
www.halcraft.com

Hirschberg Schutz and Co.
650 Liberty Avenue
Union, NJ 07083
908-810-1111
charms/embellishments

Lindstrom Tools
1440 West Taft Avenue
Orange, CA 92865
714-921-9950
beading tools
www.lindstromtools.com

**Marvin Schwab, The Bead
Warehouse**
2740 Garfield Avenue
Silver Spring, MD 20910
301-565-0487
*beads, gems, precious metal
findings, stringing materials, tools*
www.thebeadwarehouse.com

Offray Ribbon
Berwick Offray LLC
Bomboy Lane and Ninth Street
Berwick, PA 18603
800-237-9425
ribbon

Phoenix Beads, Jewelry and Parts
5 West 37th Street
New York, NY 10018
212-278-8688
*imported glass, gemstone, pearl and
crystal beads*
www.phoenixbeads.com

Paula Radke Dichroic Glass
P.O. Box 1088
Morro Bay, CA 93442
800-341-4945
dichroic beads
www.paularadke.com

Rings and Things
P.O. Box 450
Spokane, WA 99210
800-336-2156
*beads, tools, findings, stringing
materials*
www.rings-things.com

Serena's Beadery
*online retailer of beads and beading
supplies*
www.serenasbeadery.com

Swarovski North America Limited
1 Kenney Drive
Cranston, RI 02920
800-463-0849
*Swarovski crystal beads,
components*

Thunderbird Supply
1907 West Historic Route 66
Gallup, NM 87301
800-545-7968
*beads, findings, gemstones, tools,
stringing materials*
www.thunderbirdsupply.com

York Novelty
10 West 37th Street
New York, NY 10018
800-223-6676
Czech glass beads
www.yorkbeads.com

INDEX

ACKNOWLEDGMENTS

'To bead or not to bead?' is only ever asked by those who have not yet fallen
under the magic spell of beading, which surrounds and colors your life from
the start. Once you have started beading you will never utter those words
again, because you will be too busy beading! Create your rainbows
and give life to your dreams

Special thanks must go to the following companies who always go
the extra mile for me when searching for that elusive product:

Karen and Andy at Beads Direct who are my local bead company
and really were always there and encouraged me.

Romy at Viking Loom who searches the world for fabulous beads.

Dan at Scientific Wire who I blame for all this, for having such
a good product and service.

Anne Dillon who made me a range of beautiful polymer clay
beads used as a fastener in the wire knitted section.

Serena at Serenas beadery over there in South Dakota for
all her beautiful beads.

Barry at Caravan Beads in America for his cheerful
emails and enthusiasm.

I would also like to thank the following:

Cindy, my publisher, who saw what I could do and inspired me to 'catch hold
of my star' and to all her colleagues who work so hard.

Geoff Dann and Gloria Nicol for great photography
and fun photo sessions

My darling husband Nigel who is my world and my rock and whose patience
with me and all things beady has been great. who makes me laugh every day
and shares my dreams.

James and Emma, my children, whose arrival in my life and the journey with
them was, and still is, great fun. They inspire me and amaze me still.

M. J. H.: you know who you are and the part you have played
in this journey. I owe you.

Take hold of your dream
Catch on to that star
Have faith in yourself
You are what you are

Chrissie Day 2005